"To a mom's sometimes rushed and chaotic world, *Mothering with Spiritual Power* comes as a light on a hill, placing us firmly on solid rock. Debra Woods delivers a deeply personal, eloquent message that is never preachy but rather manages to uplift, entertain, and empower."

—VICTORIA AKSELSEN FISHER,
Mother of three

"Motherhood, what an amazing journey! After eight years of married childlessness, I will finally get my chance at motherhood this May. I read *Mothering with Spiritual Power* and felt uplifted, encouraged, and comforted about the challenges I will soon be facing. I feel women at any stage in life can benefit from the insights shared by this talented new author."

—LINDSEY SHUMWAY,
Author of *I Chose You* and
101 Creative Dates for Latter-day Saints

"The scriptures this book uses are ones most of us are probably very familiar with, yet Debra is able to give them such a fresh, unique-to-moms perspective. It's reassuring to see how ancient scripture can be applied to modern parenting problems, and to be reminded that as different as our unique parenting challenges are, we also have much in common—including the greatest parenting advice book available: the Book of Mormon."

BRIDGET REES,
Editor for *LDS Living* magazine and mother of two

"*Mothering with Spiritual Power* is a remarkable look at some well-loved Book of Mormon scriptures applied beautifully to remind us of the power of inspiration and prayer, and the reality of the Atonement in our mothering work. With a wise, honest voice, Sister Woods draws on her own mothering experiences to show how prayerful pondering of the scriptures can give us vision to see through worldly trials to eternal goals. In *Mothering with Spiritual Power*, Sister Woods insightfully describes a scripture-based parenting style and the powerful parenting truths and clarity available to us as we attempt to liken the scriptures unto us for our profit and learning."

—LISA HAINS BARKER, PHD
Clinical Psychologist and mother of three

"Debra Woods has gleaned much from her careful reading of the Book of Mormon. With unique mothering perspective, she makes a single verse come alive in a very personal way. Her inspiring insights are powerful reminders of the importance of finding joy in motherhood and the crucial role of mothers in raising responsible children."

—DEBBIE BOWEN,
Author of *Nobody's Better Than You, Mom!* and
W.O.R.K: Wonderful Opportunities for Raising Responsible Kids

"Debra Sansing Woods uses an eloquent, articulate, and personal style to tie the Book of Mormon to the sacred role of motherhood. This book will lift the spirits and confidence of any mother. I highly recommend this book."

—RANDAL A. WRIGHT, PHD
Author of *25 Mistakes LDS Parents Make and How to Avoid Them*

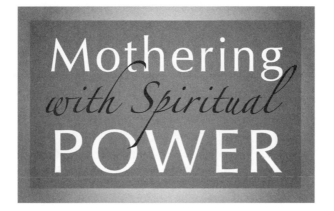

BOOK OF MORMON INSPIRATIONS
FOR RAISING A RIGHTEOUS FAMILY

Mothering *with Spiritual* POWER

BOOK OF MORMON INSPIRATIONS
FOR RAISING A RIGHTEOUS FAMILY

DEBRA SANSING WOODS

CFI
Springville, Utah

ISBN 13: 978-1-59955-059-6

Published by CFI, an imprint of Cedar Fort, Inc., 2373 W. 700 S., Springville, UT, 84663
Distributed by Cedar Fort, Inc., www.cedarfort.com

LIBRARY OF CONGRESS CATALOGING-IN-PUBLICATION DATA

Woods, Debra Sansing, 1965–
  Mothering with spiritual power : book of mormon inspirations for raising a righteous family / Debra Sansing Woods.
    p. cm.
  ISBN 978-1-59955-059-6 (alk. paper)
  1. Mothers—Religious life. 2. Mormon women—Religious life. 3. Book of Mormon—Quotations. I. Title.

  BX8641.W76 2007
  248.8'431—dc22

    2007018967

Cover design by Nicole Williams
Cover design © 2007 by Lyle Mortimer
Edited and typeset by Annaliese B. Cox

Printed in the United States of America

10 9 8 7 6 5 4 3 2 1

Printed on acid-free paper

For my mom,
Joyce Abbott Sansing,
With deepest gratitude and love.

And for my children,
Amanda, Samantha, Kelly, Charlotte, and Brady.
I am so blessed to be your mother.
I love you forever.

Contents

Acknowledgments

With admiration and appreciation:

To the first-class powerhouse publishing team at Cedar Fort: Lee Nelson for acquiring my manuscript; Heather Holm for so graciously coordinating the production of this book; Annaliese Cox for her graceful, even masterful editing of my manuscript as well as for her gorgeous typesetting and page design; Nicole Williams for her beautiful cover art; and Katie Hofheins and Angie Harris for creatively and tirelessly promoting my book. You have each made the trek to publication and beyond a true pleasure.

To four of my favorite women in the LDS publishing industry—Lindsey Shumway, Emily Watts, Bridget Rees, and Kathryn H. Kidd: Thanks for letting your lights shine so brightly through your writing and your mentoring. You have touched many, including me, with your words and wisdom, and, truth be told, you each inspire me to write like my pen is on fire.

To Anna Poole: No one could ask for a dearer, more devoted friend than you. There's no way our meeting almost two decades ago could have been just by chance. How completely blessed I have been by our friendship in the years since. You are, in sum, the ultimate cheerleader for those you love. Thanks for being my friend and, at heart, for being my sister.

To Victoria Akselsen Fisher: You are the LDS writing-and-mothering friend I had spent nearly a decade looking for before I found you. I will never cease to be amazed by your productivity: I write one book while you write four. You are an inspiration in motherhood and in writing. My kids and I look forward to seeing your wonderful fantasy youth books in print. Thanks for your encouragement and your example. Let's keep writing our way toward our dreams.

To all of my terrific mothering friends for cheering me on in my writing and, most especially, in motherhood; among them: Diana Tritapoe, Nancy Billings, Lisa Barker, Laura Skoglund, Tracy Kriese, Becky Hull, and others. I am richly and deeply blessed by your friendship.

To my sisters, Lea Giberson, Mary Ellsworth, and Becky Adling: Every year, I love you more and more. I am so thankful you are my sisters, and I am so glad we are raising our kids together even though we live, in some cases, across deserts and oceans from each other.

To my dad and mom, Bill and Joyce Sansing: For so many reasons, among the obvious, this book would never have been written without you. I thank you for loving me, for raising me in the gospel, and for teaching me and showing me, through your examples, that heartfelt dreams can come true through hard work and steady determination. I strive to honor you every day with my life and work as a mother and as a writer.

To my husband, Barry, who is the love of my life and my forever: I can imagine no more comfortable place on earth than being with you. Thanks for your steadfast support in all aspects of my life and for your complete confidence in my ability to write this book. But most of all, thanks for loving me so well; you are ever solid as a rock.

And, of course, to my children: Amanda, Samantha, Kelly, Charlotte, and Brady, who are the lights and joys of my life. Heavenly Father has blessed me beyond measure by letting me be your mother. What an amazing adventure we've had together. Thanks for sharing in my enthusiasm for this project, but more than anything, thanks for being such terrific kids overall. I love you up to the moon and back, out to all the planets in the solar system, the galaxy and beyond, and back and forth a million-billion times, at least.

LIKENING THE SCRIPTURES
UNTO OUR MOTHERING LIVES

*I did liken all scriptures unto us, that it might
be for our profit and learning.*

—1 NEPHI 19:23

I vividly recall the feelings that surfaced the moment my first daughter was placed in my arms just after she was born. Even with all the child care and parenting books I had read in the months leading up to her birth, I felt enormously unprepared for the awesome but precious responsibility that lay nestled in my arms.

Sixteen years have passed, and four more children have joined our family since that midnight birth. And I am happy to report that despite my initial and sometimes recurring doubts about myself as a mother, my children seem to be content and generally thriving.

While raising children, I have, at times, found solid support and guidance within the pages of some terrific parenting books. But, as helpful as some of those books have been, I must tell you that they do not compare in power and inspiration to the support and guidance I have found repeatedly within the pages of the Book of Mormon.

First of all, I have discovered that the simple act of feasting upon the words of the Book of Mormon brings an increased power and smoother flow to my days. On the days when I read from the Book of Mormon, I feel more in tune with the Spirit, more focused on following the Savior's example, and more committed to teaching my children the gospel in my home each day. When I read the passage in the Book of Mormon that proclaims, "For my soul delighteth in the scriptures" (2 Nephi 4:15), I recognize that I often feel that same delight in my own scripture study.

In part, I feel that same delight because of the overall effect I experience when reading from the pages of the Book of Mormon. But I also feel that delight because, almost invariably, when I read from the pages of the Book of Mormon, I run across a verse, a passage, or perhaps even an entire account that I am inspired to apply in my role as a mother.

I remember well the lightbulb moment I experienced in my seminary days when I first read these words of Nephi, "I did liken all scriptures unto us, that it might be for our profit and learning" (1 Nephi 19:23). Nephi's words served as an awakening to me to pay closer attention to what I read in the scriptures and to liken the scriptures unto my own life so they might, in fact, be for my profit and learning. And as much as I took those words to heart in my youth, I will tell you that I have taken them far more to heart during my years as a mother. After all, being a mother has asked more of me than any other work I have attempted to do at any other time in my life.

So, over the years, as I have kept a red pencil in hand while reading from the pages of the Book of Mormon, I have highlighted or underlined many verses that have made a profound difference in my mothering life. Some of my favorites include: "And Christ hath said: If ye will have faith in me ye shall have the power to do whatsoever thing is expedient in me" (Moroni 7:33), "O Lord, pour out thy Spirit upon thy servant, that he may do this work with holiness of heart" (Mosiah 18:12), and "All thy children shall be taught of the Lord; and great shall be the peace of thy children" (3 Nephi 22:13).

In recent years, I have collected many of what I have come to think of as my favorite mothering scriptures. And my list is ever growing. If I sought to share all of my favorite mothering scriptures to date, there would be far too many to contain in one book. So, here in this book, I share my thoughts and reflections on *some* of my favorite mothering scriptures. May we all seek to nourish ourselves deeply with the scriptures, adding prayer, pondering, fasting, and inspired action. And by so doing, may we tap into the immense spiritual power that the Lord can provide us with as we strive to raise our precious children.

Chapter One

CALLING OUR CHILDREN TO US ONE BY ONE

And he took their little children, one by one, and blessed them, and prayed unto the Father for them.
—3 NEPHI 17:21

I love to tell my children the story of Jesus' visit to the Americas, especially the part where he pauses in the midst of speaking to the multitudes to invite the children to come unto him, one by one, so he can bless them and pray for them. I share this story with my children so that they will have no doubts about how precious they are to the Lord. As I read this story to them, I am reminded myself of just how precious they are to me.

When I attempt to envision what it must have been like for those children during Jesus' visit, I put myself into the shoes of just one child and imagine being called forward to be in the presence of the Lord, one on one. When I think of such an experience, I am immediately enveloped with a sense of being wholly and completely loved. In such circumstances I would no doubt have felt a deep sense of confirmation of my worth as a child of God.

Of course, the child in me cannot help but wonder what the Lord would have said in my blessing and in his prayer unto the Father in my behalf had I been one of those little children. Whatever he may have said, I know that his words would have made a profound impact on me not only at the time but also, I'm sure, for the rest of my life and even for eternity.

When I shift perspectives and view Jesus' visit with the children through the eyes of a parent watching closely nearby, I cannot help but desire that my children have the opportunity to partake of such love. Although Jesus is not here in body to physically bless and pray for our children individually, he showed us the way during his time on earth to positively impact our children's lives. Through his example, he invited each of us, as parents, to call our children to us one by one, to be part of blessing them and praying unto the Father for them.

I find it particularly significant that the Lord called the children to him one by one. No one would have faulted him if he had called the children to him all together and blessed them as a group and then prayed for them as a whole. Even such an experience would have been extraordinary and would have made a lasting impression on all present. But I believe that the Lord, through his example, wanted us to know that nurturing our children collectively is not enough. Our children need us, perhaps now in this day and time as never before, to call them to us individually, to specifically focus on connecting with them, one on one, as we strive to meet their specific needs.

As the mother of five children, from a toddler to a teen, I find it challenging to make time to spend with each of my children individually on a regular basis. But I know that it's important to do so because I realize that I cannot possibly meet all of the needs of one child, say my teenage daughter, while also attending to the needs of her siblings.

I strive to take each of my children on mother/child dates in which we get to spend some uninterrupted time together doing something that we both love, whether it's going on a bicycle ride or browsing through a favorite bookstore. These outings provide wonderful opportunities for bonding and for taking a reading on my child's emotional and spiritual well-being, but they are hard to come by given the schedules and logistics of our family life. If I want to connect with each of my children in meaningful ways on a regular basis, I've learned that I must be more realistic about how I weave one-on-one time into the fabric of our days.

I'm most successful in spending one-on-one time with each of my children when I stay alert for the windows of opportunity that I could so easily miss in the midst of our busy family life. I've discovered that my fourteen-year-old daughter and I can enjoy late-evening conversations together when we share the chore of walking the dog through the neighborhood. I've also learned that I can sneak in some special time with my five-year-old daughter if I will take a break from the never-ending household chores while my toddler is sleeping and my older children are not yet home from school. I have learned that with some determination and creativity, I really can fit in some focused time with each of my kids on a regular basis.

As special as these times can be, my favorite one-on-one time with my kids is when I tuck them into bed at night. Things can be hectic in the evenings with church, school, and sports activities, but most nights, if I plan well and stay on track, I can have a few minutes of special time with each of my kids before they go to sleep. After they bathe and dress for bed, I meet them individually in their bedrooms, where we'll talk about their day and what they're looking forward to in the day to come. Sometimes we play a game where I ask, "Who loves you?" And no matter how many answers they provide, I remind them of even more people who love them. With my older children, I enjoy sharing a story from the *New Era* or even the *Ensign*. With the younger ones, I like to share a story from the *Friend* and then kneel with them as they say their personal prayers. Whatever we may talk about, whatever we may do during our time together, I try to do it with my full attention and lots of love.

During our times together, I am better able to tune into each of my children, to become more aware of their individual needs, and to know more fully how to meet those needs. Sometimes, when I've spent special time with my children, I realize that what they need most is a priesthood blessing to provide them with some extra guidance or to give them comfort. There are few experiences that touch me more than watching a worthy priesthood holder, my husband or another brother, bless my child in the Savior's name. I wish that parents everywhere knew firsthand the power of the priesthood to literally bless their children's lives. What a difference such knowledge could make.

While priesthood blessings for our children are not a daily occurrence in our home, prayers to Heavenly Father in our children's behalf are. My husband and I say these prayers in their presence during our family time together or just before we eat our meals. In saying these prayers, we strive to express gratitude for each of our children by name and to give thanks for the difference they make in our lives. We may also, in their presence, pray specifically for a need we've become aware of—whether that need is to do well on an upcoming test they have studied for or a need to know how to deal with a difficult peer at school. Then there are the prayers that my husband and I say as a couple for our children as well as my personal prayers, where I pour out my heart in detail to the Lord regarding my children. I cannot imagine raising my children without the strength, comfort, and direction these prayers provide.

The Savior made it clear through his simple but powerful example that we must make time to call our children to us, to see that they are blessed, and to pray unto our Heavenly Father for them. With such busy and sometimes stress-filled lives, we can find it challenging to make this kind of time in our homes. Even so, it is my experience that when we as parents make the effort to follow the Savior's example, we will be doing much to strengthen our families. For, in seeking to spend such meaningful time with each of our children, we will grow closer to them, and, in the process, help them to grow closer to the Lord.

Chapter Two

PARTAKING OF THE GOSPEL WITH OUR CHILDREN

> *And as I partook of the fruit thereof it filled my soul*
> *with exceedingly great joy; wherefore, I began to be*
> *desirous that my family should partake of it also;*
> *for I knew that it was desirable above all other fruit.*
> —1 NEPHI 8:12

One Saturday night, as our family was driving home from an outing, I asked my kids if any of them planned to share their testimonies in our ward's fast and testimony meeting the next day. They all replied immediately and almost in unison: "N-o-o-o-o!" It was clear to me that their negative responses meant "No way, I'm afraid to stand up in front of all those people" rather than "No way, I don't have a testimony to share, big or small."

I suppose I wasn't surprised by their answers. After all, my kids are still very much beginners at speaking in public, and that fact alone would make almost anyone feel shy about sharing something as personal and powerful as a testimony. I've had extensive public speaking experience myself and yet still feel somewhat hesitant about sharing my testimony in front of others. There are times, though, when any fears I have of publicly bearing my testimony are almost completely overridden by a deep desire to share. On our ride home that night, I knew that fast and testimony meeting the next day would be just such a time.

As I thought about my desire to share my testimony on that particular Sabbath morning, I recalled a favorite Book of Mormon verse (1 Nephi 8:12) where Lehi shares his feelings about his vision of the tree of life. When he relates his experience, I feel as if it is my experience. When he says, "And as I partook of the fruit thereof it filled my soul with exceedingly great joy," I think, *Yes, I too have felt that joy as I have partaken of the gospel of Jesus Christ. In fact, I too have felt exceedingly great joy as I have partaken.* And when Lehi goes on to say that, "[he] began to be desirous that [his] family should partake of it also," I can't help but think, *Me too! I want very much for my family to partake as well.* When Lehi gives his reasons for wanting his family to partake of the fruit (of the gospel) by saying, "For I knew that it was desirable above all other fruit," I can't help but agree, *There is nothing to compare to the gospel in desirability when we actively partake.*

Lehi's sharing of his feelings about his vision has been such a gift to me in my parenting life. Through his telling of his experience, he has inspired me to actively and enthusiastically share my beliefs with my children by sharing my testimony with them at home, in church meetings, and elsewhere.

Some may say that it was easier for Lehi in his time and circumstances to be so completely focused on sharing the gospel with his children. After all, he had very little in the way of material things to give his children during their wilderness sojourn. I am convinced, though, that even if Lehi had lived in our day and time, he would have looked beyond the pervasive materialism that runs rampant today to see that the best gifts we can give our kids exist within the gospel. His example is an invitation to each of us to remain focused on giving our children the best even in a world that seems bent on confusing us about what that best is.

I have learned firsthand that we can, if we're not careful, go through the motions of teaching the gospel to our kids without really and truly sharing it with them much at all. In my experience, this happens when we rush through our teaching and forget to savor our shared gospel experiences. When I think of partaking of the gospel with my children,

I liken it to partaking of perfectly ripe, juicy fruit together. If I share the fruit (perhaps a mango) with my family while the television blares, one of my kids chats on the phone, and several side conversations are going on at once, it is unlikely that any of us will really appreciate the full beauty and tastiness of the fruit we share.

On the other hand, if we eliminate unnecessary distractions and sit down without rushing to partake of the fruit, we will more fully enjoy sharing and savoring it together. It is even better with the gospel. If we will make a conscious effort to eliminate distractions, to slow down so we can savor the gospel as we partake of it together, we will surely share many memorable, moving, and even life-changing spiritual experiences. These shared experiences are some of the most wonderful gifts Heavenly Father has for us in family life if we will be conscious of seeking them out. As we seek them out, we and our children will surely be blessed.

I confess that, as a parent, I have always carried a secret wish—the wish that if I would do my part in sharing the gospel with my children, they would automatically follow in embracing the gospel and recognizing the full beauty and value therein. I now understand that this wish, as well-intended as it has been, is terribly naïve. After all, I have seen parents I know and respect as spiritual mentors struggle with heartache as one or more of their children have turned away from the gospel either by conscious intent or through a slow and unintentional falling away. I cannot help but recall Lehi's experience with his own sons Laman and Lemuel. He so desired for his sons to fully partake of the gospel, but, despite his most earnest pleadings and many tearful prayers, they never did.

Lehi's experience with Laman and Lemuel is a reminder to us that the Lord's perfect plan includes the gift of agency. The Lord does not force us to follow him; rather he invites us to follow him, again and again and again. During my years as a mother, I have come to better understand and appreciate the wisdom and perfection of the Lord's plan. He knows so well what we are still learning—that, as parents, we may be able to compel our children to attend church with us or to be physically present in family home evenings but that we can never compel their hearts to follow.

My young children have little say these days about whether they attend church or join us for family home evenings, but I teach them the gospel with the awareness that the choice of whether they live the gospel in their adult lives will ultimately be theirs. The time I have to teach my children the gospel hands-on before they're grown is short, so I want to make the most of it. As I have sought the Lord's guidance, I have felt impressed through the Spirit that I need to seek to have as many spiritual experiences as I can with my children while I am raising them. I have had no sense that these experiences must be complex or grand but that I must do my part, however simple, to help familiarize my children with the workings of the Spirit, to help them see the beauties of the gospel, and to feel the love of their Heavenly Father and his son, Jesus Christ.

My husband and I seek these spiritual experiences through the obvious—through church meetings, regular family scripture study, family home evenings, and so forth. But we also seek them in less formal ways, such as through impromptu discussions at the dinner table that highlight a spiritual topic or by telling a favorite scripture while we're doing chores together and sharing how that scripture has guided us in particular circumstances. My husband and I carry a prayer in our hearts to be alert to opportunities for sharing the gospel with our children because those chances can so easily be missed. Whatever forum we find for our sharing, we invite our children again and again to immerse themselves in the gospel, to see the Lord's hand in their lives, and to seek to live in tune with the Spirit.

When it comes to our children, I understand that there are no guarantees, but it is my hope that through our sharing, through my children's choices, and through the workings of the Spirit, my children will someday come to feel as Lehi did in his time and as I do now. I hope that they will choose to actively partake of the gospel throughout their lives, so much so that their souls will be filled with exceedingly great joy and that they too will be desirous that their own families will partake of the gospel. It is my hope that my children will learn for themselves what I am learning now—that the gift of the gospel is most desirable above anything our material world can possibly offer.

Chapter Three

SEEKING HOLINESS
OF HEART

> *O Lord, pour out thy Spirit upon thy servant,*
> *that he may do this work with holiness of heart.*
> —MOSIAH 18:12

Several years ago, while reading an intriguing magazine interview featuring a non-LDS mother of eight young children, I was struck by how calm and at ease with herself the mother seemed to be. I wanted to know her secret. As I read through the interview, I was amazed to learn that she managed to break away from the demands of child rearing nearly every morning to drive to a nearby monastery for a period of quiet reflection and prayer. During this meditative time, she would turn her thoughts to God and to her children and ask the Lord to make her a tool for good in her children's lives that day.

As a contemplative person myself, I hunger for such time when, in my case, I can go to the temple to be spiritually nourished and to take the time to really pause and think about each of my five kids and to commit myself to being more Christlike in my interactions with them. As beneficial as such a scenario would be, it is rare that I can find that kind of time in a given day. And, like most moms I know, even if I could find the time, I don't have the support system necessary to make such a daily or even weekly experience possible.

Even so, I strive to carve out some reflective, focused time every day, even if only for a few minutes behind closed doors, to turn to the Lord to seek his guidance and to ask for greater strength and wisdom in loving and nurturing my children. I find, not surprisingly, that the days when I slow down long enough to consciously invite the Spirit into my mothering life tend to be the very days that run more smoothly in our home.

As I've studied the scriptures over the years in an effort to seek guidance as a parent, I have found myself drawn again and again to Alma's prayer when he takes Helam into the waters to baptize him. Just before Alma performs the baptism, he cries out to the Lord, saying: "O Lord, pour out thy Spirit upon thy servant, that he may do this work with holiness of heart" (Mosiah 18:12). As a mother, I love this prayer because Alma is praying on his feet, so to speak. There is no time in this instance for a great, long pause in which Alma can collect himself and pray a lengthy, thoughtful prayer before he goes about doing his Father's work.

Like Alma, we mothers cannot always find time in our busy days to send a focused, well-thought-out prayer to heaven. If we are going to stay in tune with the Spirit, we're likely going to have to spend some time praying on our feet, whether those prayers are whispered to heaven while we're tackling a sink full of dirty dishes or comforting a fevered, restless child in the middle of the night. Alma's prayer reminds us that praying on our feet is acceptable and likely even pleasing to the Lord.

As much as I appreciate Alma's reminder that we do not have to go off to some quiet, ideal place to connect with the Lord each day, I'm even more deeply affected by the words he uses as he prays and the inspiration those words provide for me in my prayers as a mother. If I take Alma's prayer and apply it to my mothering experience, I am reminded to ask the Lord to pour out his Spirit upon me, his servant, that I may mother my children (and his children) with a holiness of heart. What this prayer lacks in length it makes up for in power. This prayer provides me with perspective. I cannot help but laugh when I think of the times I have wished to be a prettier, less frumpy mother or a funnier, savvier mom. The truth is that those things matter very little when compared to seeking to become a mother who parents her children with holiness of heart.

So, what does it mean to pray for holiness of heart as we go about the important and sacred work of raising our children? Each mother's answer to this question would likely be a bit different, but overall I imagine that most moms would pray for holiness of heart that includes being in tune with the Spirit on a daily basis. What a comforting way to raise our children—knowing that the Spirit can be with us and knowing that we can have access to divine guidance today, tomorrow, and every day yet to come if we will seek it and follow it.

In striving to mother with holiness of heart, I have prayed specifically to more fully recognize the divine natures of my children since they are indeed children of God. I have also sought, through prayer, to better appreciate and honor the individual worth of each of my children, for each one is a child unlike any other child who has ever been upon the face of the earth, with his or her own gifts and talents waiting to be nurtured and developed. Although some of the specifics in my prayers have varied over the years, all of my prayers, individually and collectively, have made a powerful and positive difference in our family life.

When I pray a prayer like Alma's, but in my own words as prompted by the Spirit, I feel an immediate sense of reverence for the work I am doing in raising my kids. There are tough days in parenting to be sure. Every seasoned parent knows this. Even so, I have great faith that the Lord will help each of us as mothers, if we will turn to him, to raise our children in righteousness and in an abundance of love. With his help, we can become the kind of mothers he wants us to be, the kind of mothers who consistently and joyfully strive to raise their children with holiness of heart.

Chapter Four

FORGIVING OURSELVES
FOR OUR SHORTCOMINGS

> *And there came a voice unto me, saying: Enos, thy*
> *sins are forgiven thee, and thou shalt be blessed. And I,*
> *Enos, knew that God could not lie; wherefore, my guilt*
> *was swept away. And I said: Lord, how is it done?*
> *And he said unto me: Because of thy faith in Christ.*
> —ENOS 1:5–8

I remember well the afternoon when I was baptized as a newly turned eight-year-old. I felt dressed for heaven in the lovely white-eyelet dress my mother had made especially for the occasion. To me, my dress represented just how clean and perfect I would be the moment I rose out of the water, freshly washed from sin, a newly baptized child of God. On my baptismal day, I was filled with high ideals and an incomplete understanding of the gospel. And, as such, I promised myself that I would behave perfectly from the moment I was baptized on through forevermore.

It probably came as a surprise to no one except me that things didn't go according to plan. After my baptism, I returned home with my family, changed into my play clothes, and headed outside to play on the swing set with two of my sisters. Things were going well—that is, until my older sister and I decided that we each wanted to be on the slide at the same moment. I don't remember all the details of our squabble, but I do remember that what started as an exchange of harsh words quickly descended into a vigorous bout of pushing and shoving. Not able to take it any longer, I broke away from the scene, tears streaming down my face, and walked into the house. I was devastated, not so much by the fact that I had lost control of the slide to my older sister (although this fact alone was fairly upsetting) but because I had blown my earnest goal of being perfect forevermore. And saddest of all, I had blown it in just the hour or so after my baptism.

As dismal as things seemed at the time, I am happy to report that all was not lost that day. In the years following my baptism, with the help of a surprising number of other imperfect moments, I learned much about the repentance process, including forgiveness of self and others. And I gained what I thought, at the time, was a solid understanding and appreciation of the Savior's Atonement and the part his Atonement can play in our lives as we strive for perfection.

A funny thing happened, though, when I became a mom. Almost all of the lessons I had learned about forgiveness of self went out the window with the birth of my first child. As it turns out, my experience of becoming a mom was, in some ways, like my experience of becoming newly baptized. As a newly baptized eight-year-old, I had naïvely held a notion something to this effect: "I am baptized now. I am perfect. I will not make mistakes." And after the birth of my first child, despite my age and experience, I held an equally naïve notion: "I am a mother now, so I'm supposed to be perfect. I will try not to make any mistakes at all."

This probably won't come as a surprise to any veteran moms, but things didn't go according to plan. Thankfully, I didn't make any major mistakes during my first few hours of motherhood. But, truth be told, I have probably more than made up for that slow start in the years since.

Despite my earnest efforts, my shortcomings and failings over the years have been numerous. Among them, there have been the times when I have lost my patience and yelled cross words at my children, the times when we have missed holding family home evenings and family scripture study sessions, as well as the occasions when one of my children has needed a listening ear and I have failed them miserably with my wandering thoughts.

From my discussions with other mothers, I know that I'm not the only mom who struggles along the path of motherhood, sometimes feeling like I'm making more than my share of mistakes. Nor am I the only mom who struggles to forgive herself when she comes up short.

A few mornings ago, I felt especially discouraged when I fell far beneath my potential as a mother. It was a school morning, and as usual, my children and I were racing to get through our morning routine before the school bus arrived. My six- and nine-year-old daughters had each asked me to fix their hair. I usually enjoy styling any one of my daughter's hair—braiding it or brushing it into a ponytail—because such an interaction provides me with a brief but meaningful opportunity to nurture that daughter hands-on. So, when my daughters ask me to fix their hair, I only ask in return that they comply with three simple rules: they brush their own tangles out, they bring their own brush with them (as opposed to another family member's), and they wait patiently for their turn.

On this particular morning, my six- and nine-year-old raced toward me while fighting over a brush—my brush, no less—and each hollering, "Me first, me first!" To make matters worse, neither of them had combed the tangles out of their hair, and we were running well behind schedule. As I tried to reach out to retrieve my brush and bring order to the chaos, my nine-year-old daughter grabbed the brush away from her younger sister and hurled it across the room where it slammed against the wall with a crack and landed on the floor, broken in two. My daughter, instead of going to retrieve my brush and apologize for her impulsive actions, left the room without a word to go in search of her own brush, the brush she should have brought in the first place. I know this daughter well enough to understand that her seeming indifference was a cover for her own surprise and disappointment at what she had done. Even so, it irked me that there had been no apologies, just a mad dash to get on with the morning preparations before the bus arrived.

I could have and should have talked with both of the daughters involved about what had happened—what their actions were, how I felt about no longer having a usable brush, what they could do to make amends and to do better next time, and so on. But I didn't. Instead, I asked my nine-year-old for her brush. She handed it over, thinking, I'm sure, that I would use it to fix her hair. Instead, I asked her how she would feel if someone broke her brush. Then, surprising even myself, I snapped her brush in two. I hadn't intended to do such a thing and felt instantly regretful and miserable over my actions.

Rather than doing the things that would have lifted my children and me up from a low point in our morning, I had acted impulsively in a way that had sunk us to an even lower point. No one felt worse about this than I did. I apologized immediately for my actions and expressed sorrow over what I had done. I told my daughter that I would replace her brush and, not wanting to let her completely off the hook, asked her to come up with a solution for replacing my broken brush. Somehow, even in the midst of all the drama, my kids managed to get ready for school and head out the door to catch the bus.

The events of that early weekday morning had definitely cast a shadow over what should have been a good day. Thoroughly ashamed of my actions, I resolved not to let such a thing happen again. Even with all the power of my resolutions, I still felt blue. I found myself recalling numerous other mistakes I had made as a mom over the years and all the ways I hadn't measured up to my ideal of motherhood. I felt down and discouraged and not sure how to pick myself up.

Several days later, as I climbed the stairs to deliver some freshly folded laundry to my children's bedrooms, a picture at the top of the stairs caught my attention. It was a picture of the Savior. My eleven-year-old daughter had hung it there some months earlier. Whenever I see that picture, I feel as if the Savior himself is looking directly at me and reminding me of just how precious my little ones are to him and how I should seek to love them as he would love them himself.

On this particular day, I felt that usual reminder, but I felt something else as well. When I looked at the picture of the Savior, I felt as if he were saying to me, "I am here to remind you to be kind to your children, but I am also here to remind you to be kind to yourself." How, I wondered, would the Lord want me to be kinder to myself? As I pondered this question, a simple but powerful thought came to mind: the Lord would want me to be kinder to myself by learning to forgive myself more readily when I make mistakes in mothering my children. But how, I wondered, could I learn to better forgive myself when I sometimes fall so far short of my own expectations? And then, like a bolt of lightening had struck, I knew what I needed to do; I needed to open my heart more fully to the gift of the Savior's Atonement. After all, the Lord has promised to forgive me if I sincerely repent of my wrongdoings. And, if he can forgive me, surely I can forgive myself.

The scriptures make it very clear that the Lord is indeed willing to forgive us when we sincerely repent. I am reassured of this when I read scriptural passages such as, "I, the Lord, forgive sins, and am merciful unto those who confess their sins with humble hearts" (D&C 61:2) and "But as oft as they repented and sought forgiveness, with real intent, they were forgiven" (Moroni 6:8).

Sometimes I do very well at going through all the necessary steps in the repentance process—from admitting my wrongdoing to graciously accepting the Lord's forgiveness. But other times, for whatever reason, I am especially hard on myself when I have erred and end up getting stuck in the mode of berating myself for the mistake I have made. This was certainly the case when I broke my daughter's brush. I am learning, though, that getting stuck in such a mode of unwillingness to forgive myself serves no one because it leaves me feeling nothing but down and discouraged. And when I feel so down on myself, I am not as good at being the mother my children need me to be.

I want very much to be a good mother to my children, to pass the pure love of Christ on to them. But, to do this, I realize that I need to open my heart more fully to the Savior's pure love for me. And not just when I feel I am doing well as a mother, but when I fall short as well. The Lord does not expect us to be perfect forevermore once we are baptized or when we become mothers. He knew that we would make mistakes, and so, long ago, he paid the price for our sins. It seems silly to me now that I would ever go through all the work of the repentance process only to stop short of allowing myself to accept the Lord's forgiveness.

In the future, when I am in need of a gentle push forward in the repentance process to the part where I open my heart to receive the Lord's forgiveness, I will turn to Enos's account of his own repentance process and the Lord's forgiveness of him. In his account, Enos reports that after many hours of humble prayer, "there came a voice unto me, saying: Enos, thy sins are forgiven thee, and thou shalt be blessed. And I, Enos, knew that God could not lie; wherefore, my guilt was swept away. And I said: Lord, how is it done? And he said unto me: Because of thy faith in Christ" (Enos 1:5–8).

I understand now that the choice of how to proceed when we make mistakes in mothering our children is really up to us. We can choose to spend all of our time beating ourselves up for the mistakes we make (thus dragging ourselves and our children down), or we can choose to follow Enos's example of opening our hearts to the Lord's forgiveness when we have sincerely repented.

Let us follow Enos's example and choose to do the kind thing for ourselves and our children. Let us remember that God does not lie. If we will exercise faith in Christ (not just believing in him but believing in his promises too) and sincerely repent of our sins, we can trust that God will forgive us and our guilt will be swept away. And, instead of being filled with guilt, we will be filled with the pure love of Christ—a love which we can, in turn, pass on to the precious children who have been entrusted to our care.

Chapter Five

CREATING A JOYFUL
MOTHERING LIFE

> *Adam fell that men might be; and men are,*
> *that they might have joy.*
> —2 NEPHI 2:25

This scriptural passage made an enormous impact on me when I first memorized it as a seminary student more than twenty years ago. I knew then that the truth it conveyed would serve as a guiding force for me throughout the rest of my life. Previously, I had understood that our earthly life is a test and that we must endure to the end, but I hadn't—until I became familiar with this scripture—truly caught the vision that we are here to have joy even as we take our test and as we seek to endure to the end.

With this scripture in mind, I firmly believe that *we as mothers are, that we might have joy.* When I ponder this truth, I can't help but ask— am I living up to my capacity for joy as the mother to my children? Or, truth be told, is there more room for happiness in my daily life as a mother than I am currently experiencing? While I can honestly say that I'm a content mom on the whole, I must admit that, yes, there is room for more happiness in my daily life.

With these thoughts in mind, I find myself wondering—what do I know for sure about creating a joyful mothering life? First, I know that I am happiest as a mom when I make getting sufficient spiritual nourishment a priority in my daily life. When my need for spiritual nourishment goes unmet for more than a few days, I tend to grow somewhat restless and even a bit blue.

I don't set out to neglect my spiritual well-being. Rather, such neglect occurs when I become so busy doing good things for my family and friends that I leave little or no time for taking spiritual care of myself. This has definitely been the case recently as my family and I hosted an amazing number of overnight guests (thirty in all)—family and friends—during one month. We enjoyed our company immensely, every bit of it, but I confess that I had been so busy visiting with loved ones and friends, tidying the house, stocking the refrigerator, and preparing meals that I'd let my need for focused, sustained scripture study and unrushed prayers fall almost completely by the wayside. I became so anxiously engaged in doing good things for others that I'd let my spiritual well run dry. And when my spiritual well runs dry, my capacity for joy seems to shrink by a rather surprising amount.

So this week, as I seek to replenish my well, to restore my equilibrium, to lift my spirits, it is clear to me that I need to start by getting some solid spiritual nourishment. As I return to feasting upon the scriptures and praying more focused, heartfelt prayers, I start to feel like my better self again—buoyant, energetic, optimistic, and even calm. This shouldn't be surprising given the benefits I consistently find in regular and focused scripture study. The scriptures help me to stay in tune with the Lord. They smooth off the rough edges to my days and help me to better navigate whatever challenges arise along the way. When I replenish my spiritual well after a dry spell, I cannot help but feel a more genuine and grounded happiness than I have felt in a while, and, best of all, I can see my increased happiness reflected back to me in the faces of my children.

Sometimes we as moms are prone to thinking that giving any real thought to our own happiness is selfish—that it's okay to make sure that our children are happy, that our husbands are happy, and that our friends and extended family are happy, but that it is somehow not okay to give our own happiness any direct consideration. This notion seems silly to me when I recall that we are here on earth to have joy. Considering our own happiness even as we consider the happiness of those around us is a gift we give ourselves and those we love. After all, we have all heard it said that happy moms make for happy families.

When it comes to cultivating happiness in my life, I find it helpful to keep in mind the scripture that says, "This is joy which none receiveth save it be the truly penitent and humble seeker of happiness" (Alma 27:18). Are we as mothers the humble seekers of happiness spoken of in this scripture? I wish I could answer without reservation that, "Yes, I am a humble seeker of happiness," but the truth is that while I strive to be a humble seeker of happiness, I am sometimes my own greatest stumbling block when it comes to creating a truly joyful mothering life.

I find that I tend to trip myself up when I have unrealistic expectations of myself as a mom and of motherhood in general. In my early years as a mother, I went through a phase where I was particularly hard on myself. I felt that I should be accomplishing so much more in my home and with my children than I seemed capable of doing. Why, I wondered, couldn't I keep a consistently tidy home? Why couldn't I manage to get by on less sleep without being cranky when there was so much to be done each day? Why didn't I possess more talents and skills to use in family and home life than I seemed to naturally possess? I could put together a strict but manageable family budget and keep an up-to-date check register, but when it came to decorating birthday cakes or creating a beautiful and well-coordinated home interior, I felt like a serious underachiever who was completely lacking in talent

While I have benefited from developing some skills in these areas over the years, I've also benefited from learning that I sometimes need to revise my expectations of myself as a mom. In doing so, I have come to realize that my children will survive quite well without a mother-decorated birthday cake (a bakery-decorated cake seems to fill in nicely) and that while I don't have a degree in interior design, there's a lot to be said for the difference a simple can of paint can make to a child's bedroom. When I recognize and revise my unnecessarily unrealistic expectations of myself, my frustration level decreases and my overall satisfaction as a mom increases.

During the last few years, I have learned to not only revise my expectations of myself when appropriate but to sometimes go a step further and revise my expectations of motherhood in general. I went into motherhood with some pretty romantic notions about what being a mom would be like. I certainly thought that raising kids would be easier than I have found it to be. I also naïvely imagined that every day with my little ones would be almost effortlessly filled with joy.

During a period when I found myself especially pondering my hands-on experience of motherhood as compared to my expectations of what motherhood would be like, Shayla, a sister in my ward, shared a valuable insight that woke me up, an insight that has stayed with me and shaped my mothering experience ever since. She shared her thoughts that while motherhood is not a perfect experience, we are each blessed every day to experience perfect moments with our children. Yes, she was right, I realized, feeling the truth of what she shared. While motherhood is not perfect, we have the opportunity to share many beautiful and perfect moments with our children every day. We just need to be awake to those moments and attuned to them so we can more fully embrace and enjoy them.

In striving to be a humble seeker of happiness, I sometimes pause to ask myself—what can I do today to invite more genuine joy into my life and into my children's lives? More times than I am comfortable admitting, the answer has been that I need a spiritual tune-up. The bright side to this answer is that when it comes, I know exactly what steps I need to take; very simply, I need to get back to the basics of meaningful daily scripture study and more meditative prayers. Other times, I find that the answer is that I need to revise my expectations of myself, my children, or of motherhood in general. And yet, other times, the answer turns out to be something like building a stronger social network of mothering friends or carving out time in which to pursue a personal interest such as reading or family history research.

There are some moms who, despite their best efforts at seeking happiness, find such happiness to be elusive. In some instances, they may be experiencing postpartum depression. In other instances, the depression may be something they've dealt with much of their lives because of a chemical imbalance or some serious unresolved issues from their past. Depression is not something to be ashamed of, but it is certainly something to be addressed head-on, and sooner rather than later. Prayerfully seeking professional help, tapping into the love and support of understanding family members and friends, and remaining hopeful can make an important difference for a mom and her children.

There are times in all of our lives when we as moms are unlikely to be giddy with joy. After all, this life is a test, and we will experience trials and afflictions—some short-lived and others for the remainder of our lives. So, while we are unlikely to experience never-ending joy in our mothering lives, we can become conscious of embracing the happiness that comes our way and be part of actively creating the happiness that we can experience and share with our children.

I have long felt that our lives here on earth are truly gifts from our Father in Heaven and that what we do with our lives become our gifts of thanks to him in return. What better way to thank Heavenly Father than to become humble seekers of happiness who strive to create the most meaningful, joyful lives that we possibly can on earth as we raise our children. And what better gift to give our children than to give them, through our examples, permission to create genuinely happy lives themselves.

Chapter Six

REMEMBERING THE
BY-SMALL-AND-SIMPLE-THINGS
PHILOSOPHY

> *Now ye may suppose that this is foolishness in me;*
> *but behold I say unto you, that by small and simple*
> *things are great things brought to pass; and small*
> *means in many instances doth confound the wise.*
> —ALMA 37:6

By nature, I like to plow in and tackle a task without stopping when there is something that needs to be done, whether it is cleaning the house, paying the bills, or fixing a meal. While this drive-to-the-finish-line approach to getting things done served me well in my pre-parenting days, it doesn't work so well for me anymore. My children can hardly be expected to wait until Mom gets everything done before they get any attention. After all, if a baby needs a diaper change, it's best to change it immediately; if a five-year-old sustains an injury in play, attending to her right away rather than later is definitely called for; and if a teen needs a ride to an almost-forgotten church activity that started five minutes ago, I prefer to jump in the car as soon as possible and head out rather than waiting until it's convenient for me.

As a person who likes to get things done, I used to find the constant start-and-stop of motherhood especially frustrating. Over the years, though, I've adjusted to the realities of family life and have come to think of mothering as its own form of meditation. Being a mother has taught me to focus not necessarily on what I had originally intended to do but rather on what needs to be done most at this moment, whether it's that diaper change or a quick drive to the church. This shift in perspectives has made an enormous difference in my experience of family life. Even so, this shift alone has not been enough to help me master the art of balancing the hands-on mothering of my children with my desire and even my need to spend time on other things—whether those other things include tidying the house, developing a talent of my own, or spending some quality and much-needed uninterrupted time with my husband.

Where the Mothering-as-a-Meditation philosophy falls short, I have found through prayerfully seeking inspiration that the By-Small-and-Simple-Things-Are-Great-Things-Brought-to-Pass philosophy picks up. I'm embarrassed to admit that it took me several years into motherhood to fully recognize the value of embracing the By-Small-and-Simple-Things philosophy as a mom. Before I had kids I was so dazzled by the big and sustained efforts that produced quick results and instant satisfaction that the idea of doing small and simple things to get anything done hardly seemed the way to go. But as a mother for close to fifteen years now, I've learned that sometimes the only way to get anything done alongside caring for my kids is by doing those small and simple things.

Once I finally caught on to the benefits of the By-Small-and-Simple-Things approach to getting things done, I began to make it a game, to see how many ways I could use this philosophy to get things done and to make a positive difference in my family life. I have to tell you that after several years of serious experimentation, the possibilities for getting things done by using the By-Small-and-Simple-Things philosophy seem to be endless. This philosophy has worked for me in almost every facet of my mothering life—from making time for personal and meaningful scripture study to sustaining a close and connected relationship with my husband.

I first used the By-Small-and-Simple-Things philosophy in my efforts to keep a moderately tidy house with little ones underfoot. I have never been an immaculate housekeeper and likely never will be, but I strive to keep enough order in our home that I can find things when I need them and so company can drop by unexpectedly on most days without too much embarrassment.

When my children were very young, I became easily frustrated in my efforts to keep house. I naïvely and stubbornly expected to be able to complete any household task I set my mind to without stopping once I started it. It didn't take long to realize that completing tasks while raising children would be an ongoing challenge. Just thinking about this reality left me feeling discouraged.

In my search for solutions, I ran across a talk on tape by Bonnie McCullough, author of *Totally Organized*, in which she stated that a wise man once said, "By small and simple things are great things brought to pass." She then told of her experiences as a young mother to five children under five and how she learned out of necessity some small and simple but effective ways to keep house while caring for kids. Following her example, I have learned to surrender the notion of the big, sustained efforts for big, quick results and to embrace, instead, the difference that cleaning a room, any room, in my home for just five or ten minutes a day can make.

Over the years, I've also discovered that the By-Small-and-Simple-Things philosophy can make a big difference in my relationship with my husband. We are so involved in raising our children, providing a living for our family, and serving in various capacities outside our home that our marriage, as much as we love each other, can fall easily into a state of neglect. We seem to do well on very low maintenance for a time, but then the lack of care takes its toll and I find myself wondering, "Who is this handsome stranger who's helping me to raise my kids?"

In an effort to keep this from happening, my husband and I strive to stay connected in simple ways—by pausing for a hug and a quick check-in when one of us arrives home after being away, by trying to give ourselves at least a little time each evening to touch base as a couple after the children are in bed, by trying to go on one real date most weeks, and by kneeling together beside our bed for a shared prayer each night before we go to sleep. I tell my husband that he's a keeper, and we've learned together that the best way to keep each other is through our commitment to doing the small and simple things that can make a big and sustained difference in our married life.

My two great passions in life are my family and my writing. I love to read other people's writing, and I love to do my own writing. Even so, several years ago I became enormously frustrated with trying to squeeze writing time into the midst of a busy family life. I decided that maybe I was supposed to sacrifice my writing for the sake of my family. I shared these thoughts with my husband, and he expressed his doubts because he saw the joy that writing brought to me and hence to our family. I took my concerns to the Lord and told him that as much as I loved to write, I would give it up while raising my kids if that is what he wanted me to do. The Lord's answer to me was that I was not to give up my writing, that he wanted me to let my light shine through my writing, but that I had to be extra creative in how I fit writing time into my family life.

So, acting on this inspiration, I developed the "sneaky snippet" approach to getting my writing done. I sometimes sneak writing into the very early mornings and other times into the late evenings. I also sneak it in when my children are contentedly napping or playing and the times when my husband can be the hands-on dad to our kids while I slip away to the library for an hour or two. I've learned to sneak writing in whenever and however I can in ways that I believe enhance my family life rather than take away from it. While I have yet to produce a large body of work, I am a contented writing mom whose completed pieces are slowly but surely adding up.

I know many moms who have learned the secret of doing the small and simple things to bring great things to pass in their lives. One of my friends used this secret to teach herself to play the piano while her children were still very young. She trained them to let her have twenty to thirty minutes every day to sit at the piano to practice. They could stand or sit beside her but could not, unless there was an urgent need, demand her attention or touch the piano. She accomplished not just one but several significant things over time by taking this approach— she learned to play the piano well enough to play Church hymns, she instilled a love for music in her children, and she taught them the importance of respecting others.

I would like to say that by now I've learned how to get everything done that needs to be done and that I want to do, but that wouldn't be true. I get a lot done most days, to be sure, but there are still days when I find it challenging to get anything done at all. On such days when I find myself feeling especially frustrated, I've learned to stop long enough to take a deep breath, or maybe four or five, and to check in with the Lord as I strive to make a reasonable plan for getting things done. The Lord's answers to my inquiries vary according to my needs and his will for me, but one aspect to his answers almost never changes—his consistent reminder that by small and simple things are great things brought to pass.

Chapter Seven

TEACHING LOVE
AND SERVICE

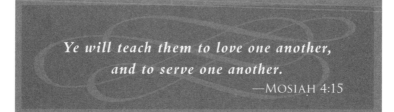

*Ye will teach them to love one another,
and to serve one another.*
—MOSIAH 4:15

What is the most important thing you want to teach your children?" An extended family member asked me this question several years ago in the middle of a conversation about something totally unrelated to kids. I was caught off guard by her question but immediately began to answer, "I want to teach my children to love—" Before I could finish, I was cut off by my relative, who exclaimed, "Oooh, that's so vague, so . . ."

I cannot recall the details of her response, but I remember feeling at the time that I should have been ashamed of my answer, that my answer seemed rather silly and lame to her. I attempted to explain my response, to fill in the details of why it is so important to me to teach my children to love the Lord and to love their neighbor (whether that neighbor is a sibling, a friend, or an acquaintance) and how I work to teach that love as something concrete and active rather than as some vague notion or feeling. Despite my best efforts, my attempts to explain were brushed aside and the subject was changed.

Feeling a bit down about the conversation, I related the experience to my husband. His response was quick but tender and powerful. "Debra, what does the New Testament teach us about love?" As I pondered his question, he shared the Savior's teachings on love, " 'Jesus said unto him, Thou shalt love the Lord thy God with all thy heart, and with all thy soul, and with all thy mind. This is the first and great commandment. And the second one is like unto it, Thou shalt love thy neighbor as thyself' (Matthew 22:37–39)." I felt an immediate lifting of my spirits. The Holy Ghost bore witness to the truth of what my husband shared. My answer had not been so silly or lame after all. In fact, it had been in sync with some of the Savior's most important teachings during his time on earth. I felt affirmed in my desire to teach my children to love the Lord and their fellow men.

Although I felt supported in my priorities by my husband and the Savior's teachings, the experience with my relative sparked a period of exploration and conversation within my own mind and heart. I pondered how we as parents can best teach our children about love as a gospel principle and as an active force in their lives rather than as some vague feeling or notion. After much thought, I have come to believe that the only way to really teach our children about love is to teach them about service. After all, it seems to me that service is love made visible. We can do much good by speaking words of love to our family and friends, but it is only through our actions, our doing, that love speaks fully.

As parents, we begin to teach our children, through our examples, about love and service on the first day they come into our lives. From the start, they ask a lot of us with their needs for nourishment and hands-on care. And we seek to meet those needs through innumerable hours of service and with a great deal of love. As our children grow older, they continue to need us, although the specifics of their needs change. As I write this, my oldest daughter seems most in need of my services as a taxi driver to and from her myriad activities. I don't mind all the driving because I find our rides together to be a clear manifestation of the statement, "In giving, you receive." By giving my daughter the rides she needs, I receive the gift of staying connected with her through the conversations we share during those rides.

I want in my heart to be loving and of good cheer whenever I am in the service of my children, and yet the reality (for me, anyway) is that I am not always my best self when caring for my kids. I suppose I shouldn't be too hard on myself about this. After all, parenthood asks of us what no other responsibility asks—that we be on duty or at least on-call twenty-four hours a day every day for eighteen years at a minimum, and that's if we have just one child.

So, yes, there are times when I don't feel very loving as a parent (perhaps I'm overwhelmed with fatigue or in need of a break to catch my breath), but I need and want to act lovingly nonetheless in serving my children. At times like this, I draw upon the power of Moroni's words when he counsels, "Wherefore, my beloved brethren, pray unto the Father with all the energy of heart, that ye may be filled with this love [meaning the pure love of Christ]" (Moroni 7:48). Whenever I have paused to pray to be filled with a purer love for my children, the Lord has blessed me. Sometimes the change in mood or the change in tone is subtle, but it is still felt. Other times, the change in heart is profound and deeply affects my children and me.

The prayer I say most often in seeking to be filled with the love of Christ is to see my children as Christ sees them. This prayer has never failed to produce a positive change in my heart. For as we seek to see our children—or anyone else for that matter—through the Savior's eyes, he opens our eyes to a clearer vision of how precious they are, how truly lovable they are, even on the days when we're not at our best.

We live in a world where we could easily become confused on how best to show our children love (and thereby teach them how to love too). The world would have us think that money can buy love, that by buying our children things—a car, new clothes, their own computer— we will be buying them the sense that they are loved. But, the thing that our children need the most, more than anything we can buy them, is our time and undivided attention.

This is the most important service we can render our children, for it is only by giving our children time and attention that we can truly come to know them and love them fully. A child who grows up with a wealth of things that money can buy may still feel a profound lack of love, but a child who grows up with an abundance of their parents' time and attention will feel a wealth of love regardless of any lack of things.

It is true that we teach our children about love and service through our examples, but our teaching would be far from complete if we did not actively invite them to love and serve others as well. Our children's best opportunities for learning to love and serve likely exist within the walls of our own homes. We encourage our children to see their siblings through the Savior's eyes. We've had discussions on more than a few occasions where we contemplate the question, "How do you think the Savior sees your brother or sister?" Another question usually follows: "How do you think Jesus would treat your brother or sister in such circumstances?" Not surprisingly, as our children get older, their answers to these questions grow more thoughtful and more caring overall.

My husband and I strive to teach our children that love calls for action and that the best way to take action is through giving service. We invite our children to give service at home in a variety of ways— by using an organized chore system, by becoming secret buddies who perform kind acts of service for each other, by inviting our children to serve along with us as we serve other family members, and by encouraging our kids to be on the lookout themselves for ways they can serve each other.

As a mother, I am delighted when I see my children catch the spirit of loving and serving each other. I recall with particular fondness the times when one of my children has been sick and another child has chosen to play nurse to the sick one. I feel a deep sense of satisfaction as I watch the healthy child do everything they can to comfort their sick sibling: bringing a glass of juice, providing blankets, and reading a story or two. I have also been blessed to be the beneficiary of my children's kind services when they've volunteered to make my bed, to watch the baby, or to fix a meal without being asked.

One thing I've noticed is that my children are beginning to carry the spirit of Christlike love and service out of our home and into their schools and the community. I feel joy when a teacher tells me about how one of my kids assisted another child in their reading or comforted a classmate when they were feeling down. Our family is not perfect in our efforts to love and serve in our home or away from home, but we are learning together better every day how to follow the Lord's admonition to love and serve one another.

When I think about the things that the gospel teaches us are important in this life versus the things the world tells us are important, I cannot help but recall a poster that was popular about the time I graduated from college. The poster featured a sleek, black luxury car and the words, "He who dies with the most toys wins." I felt sad when I read those words. They left me feeling profoundly empty. Such a philosophy, even if it was partially in jest, seemed to miss the point of our being here on earth.

In response to that poster, I've created a poster in my own imagination—one that conveys a very different message. My poster features various snapshots of a family serving together. Perhaps in one frame, a sister is seen helping a younger brother with his homework. In another, two teen siblings are volunteering at a Special Olympics event. And in yet another frame the entire family is visiting a nursing home together. The tagline in my imagined poster reads, "He who shares lots of love and care can't help but win in the ways that matter most." The scriptures make it clear that we as parents have a responsibility to teach our children to love and to serve others. This is not always easy, but as we seek to do our part to teach our children to love and to serve, I am convinced that we and our children will indeed win in the ways that matter most.

Chapter Eight

SEEKING THE POWER WE NEED TO DO THE LORD'S WILL

> *And Christ hath said: If ye will have faith in me ye shall have power to do whatsoever thing is expedient in me.*
> —MORONI 7:33

I'm sure that somewhere along the way, someone told me how much work raising kids can be. Even so, looking back I can only say that I had no idea. How could I have known? Watching other mothers care for their young children in the few years before I had kids afforded me only the smallest peek into the labor and the love involved. I could have begun motherhood better informed, I'm sure, if I had paid more attention to the work my mother did for my three sisters and me while we were growing up. She taught us much about how to care for our home and each other, but she never asked as much of us as she asked of herself. What I realize now is that my mother's almost nonstop work of caring for home and family was viewed by me then as the comforting backdrop of my sometimes self-centered childhood.

As a mother myself for almost fifteen years now, I marvel at everything my mom managed to do for us while raising us—the dresses she custom-designed and sewed for us as well as the many school, sports, and church activities she supported us in—and she did all of this while also meeting our basic needs for food and a safe, clean shelter. What amazes me most is that my mother was able to accomplish all of this despite the fact that my father was often away meeting the demands of his military career.

I never would have fully appreciated what it takes to raise children if I had not had the opportunity to become a mother myself. As challenging as I sometimes find motherhood to be, I would not trade the experience of raising my kids for anything—not for the promising career I left behind as a corporate controller or for an entire year filled with good-nights' sleep. I am very thankful to be the mother to my children. On the good days and the bad I am also thankful to know that Heavenly Father is mindful of each of us as mothers, that we can have the best possible support available to us if we will seek it.

I think that what surprised me most during my early days as a mom was the sheer physical labor involved and the almost constant sacrificing of my wants (for a full-night's sleep, a little quiet to gather my thoughts, some uninterrupted time in which to complete a task) so I could meet the very real and pressing needs of my babies. Going into motherhood, I naïvely imagined that I would always find it easy to nurture my little ones in a spirit of total love and with nothing but patience. I hadn't contemplated the times when I would feel overwhelmed with fatigue and even stressed in meeting the ever-present needs of my children and the never-ending demands involved in managing a household.

In my years as a mother I have grown to truly appreciate the power of the scriptures to give us the direction and support we need to care for our families. On the days when I feel like I'm falling behind, like motherhood is a marathon I'm not sure I'm up for, I love to read the scriptural passage that reminds me that Christ has said, "If ye will have faith in me ye shall have power to do whatsoever thing is expedient in me" (Moroni 7:33). I have no doubt that it is the Lord's will that we nurture our children with a consistent spirit of love and with great care and concern for their well-being—spiritually, physically, mentally, and emotionally. I also have no doubt that if we will look to the Savior and have faith in him, he will give us the strength we need to carry out his will. Looking back, I realize now that my mom knew where to seek the strength she needed to raise us. There were more than a few times when I saw her quietly studying the scriptures or kneeling at her bedside in personal prayer.

Looking to the Savior for strength has made all the difference in my daily life as a mother to my children. It has smoothed out the sometimes roller-coaster feel to my days and has given me confidence, a can-do spirit that I don't think I ever could have mustered on my own. Having the knowledge that the Lord will give us strength if we have faith in him has also helped me when I have faced specific crises in the midst of family life. I remember well feeling the strength of the Lord with me after I miscarried in the second trimester and almost lost my life in the process. I had four other kids to care for and was able, with the Lord's help, to do what I needed to do for them even as I processed the loss of my unborn child and the threat to my own life.

Some months later my husband and I were thrilled to learn that I was pregnant again, but our enthusiasm was quickly dampened when my husband lost his job and it became clear that we would have to move away from a city we loved. After several months of searching in a depressed job market, my husband was able to find work out of state. Given our financial needs, he started his job immediately while I stayed behind with the kids to finish readying our house for sale and to prepare for the upcoming move.

When I'm pregnant, I generally need lots of extra sleep, but with my husband's absence I found it difficult to sleep much at all. I lay awake night after night reviewing our tightly stretched budget over and over, trying to think of how else we might be able to stretch it just a bit more to make ends meet. When I wasn't thinking about our finances, I was brainstorming ways we could possibly sell our home in a depressed real-estate market and planning how we would handle the logistics of our move. The whole time I couldn't help but wonder how much longer it would be before we could finally join my husband.

My most challenging week during that difficult period was when I was about six months pregnant. I was sleep-starved and emotionally worn out and more than ready for some real rest. My husband had just left town after a weekend visit when one of my children became ill with the flu. She was completely miserable with fever and body aches and needed every bit of the attention and loving care I could give her. Little did I know that she would be just the first of my four kids to get sick that week. I spent much of that first night taking care of her only to awaken the next morning to find that I had another patient. This pattern repeated itself night after night and morning after morning until all of my kids were either sick or in various stages of recovery.

Thankfully, I didn't catch the flu myself. I was surprised and relieved to find that I had the calm energy and clear thinking I needed to take good care of my kids during that difficult week. If I hadn't known better, I would have wondered how I managed that week. But I do know better; the Lord was with me. I had sent many prayers to heaven that week and exercised faith in the Lord, and he blessed me with the physical, emotional, and mental strength I needed to take care of my kids, a strength I could not have mustered on my own.

My dearest mothering friends have taught me much about having faith in Christ and, through that faith, gaining the power we need to do the will of the Lord. One of my closest friends, in particular, has shown me the power of digging deep spiritually even as she has struggled most of her adult life with chronic and sometimes debilitating illness. Although raising three kids has been especially challenging for her, given her health, she has never lost faith in the Lord. In fact, her faith has increased over the years as she has consistently immersed herself in the scriptures, in earnest personal prayers, and in the words of the prophets and other inspired Church leaders. She has reminded me, through the strength of her example, that exercising faith can bring enormous spiritual power into our lives to help us better meet the needs of our dear children.

In my experience, I have found that sometimes the strength we need as parents comes easily; and other times, it seems that we must go through a prolonged period of nurturing and growing our faith to gain the strength we need to carry out the will of the Lord. Either way, the Lord is there for us. It is up to us to seek his help and to be open to receiving it.

As wonderful as parenthood can be, we are all likely to hit some rough patches along the way whether we find ourselves the parents of a frequently tantruming toddler, a teenager who's gone astray, or maybe even both. Whatever phase of parenthood we're in, whatever challenges we may be facing, the Lord is mindful of us. If we will exercise faith in him, he promises to give us the strength we need to do his will, the strength that only he can give—a strength that is greater than any we could ever find on our own.

Chapter Nine

ESTABLISHING A HOUSE
OF LEARNING

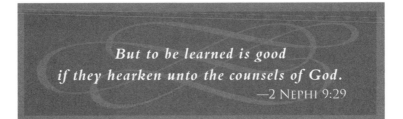

*But to be learned is good
if they hearken unto the counsels of God.*
—2 NEPHI 9:29

Several years ago, while watching a PBS documentary about motherhood, I was captivated by the interviews with various moms as they shared their thoughts on the parenting experience. As much as I enjoyed the program, I don't remember specific details about any of the moms featured except one. This particular mother stands out in my mind to this day.

I was immediately impressed with what an orderly, structured home she ran as the mother to her six children. She was a mom who was focused, energetic, and almost always in motion. Her house was immaculate, and she kept her kids on a carefully crafted schedule that they adhered to seemingly without exception.

As I watched this mother, I considered making some changes in my mothering life—a self-styled, mom-as-family-manager makeover. My thoughts ran wild with possibilities for change, so wild that I wasn't sure where to start. Even so, I was psyched and raring to go until the interview with *Super-Mom* took a turn. I heard her say something wholly unexpected and, to me, a little sad.

She related a recent conversation she had shared with a girlfriend. The friend had asked her if she had read anything interesting lately. The mom laughed in response and said something to the effect of "Are you kidding? Read? I'm the mother of six children. I haven't had time to read in at least ten years." She was serious. She didn't read . . . ever? Was that the price she paid for maintaining a spotless house and a super-ordered family life? If so, I wasn't sure I was willing to pay such a price. I couldn't fathom moving through the next ten years of my mothering life without reading a good book, even once.

Such a life sounds depressing to me because I have always had such a great love for learning and for language. Even so, in my early years as a mom, I felt overly self-indulgent and even a bit guilty when I squeezed in any time for reading and learning other than through scripture study and Church publications. Why? I'm not sure. I think I figured that a good mom meant a moving mom—one who was always in motion, either caring for her kids or managing the household. I think I was afraid that any activity that appeared leisurely, even if it gave the intellect a good workout, would make me look and feel like a lazy mom.

Even with these thoughts in mind, my desire to continue my self-education was immense. My ears perked up whenever I read a scripture or heard counsel from the pulpit that supported my deep yearning to learn. I savored the scriptures that invited me to "study and learn, and become acquainted with all good books, and with languages, tongues, and people" (see D&C 90:15) and reminded me to "seek ye out of the best books words of wisdom; seek learning, even by study and also by faith" (D&C 88:118). I was especially affected by the scriptural admonition to establish a house of learning (see D&C 88:119).

That was exactly what I wanted—a house of learning. However, I couldn't give myself permission to work wholeheartedly toward that end until I read about a General Authority who was an enthusiastic reader of good literature. He said that he did not let a day go by without reading forty or fifty pages out of a good book. I decided that if he, as a Church leader and devoted disciple, could make getting intellectual nourishment a priority, maybe it would be okay for me as a busy mom of young children to make time to satisfy my hunger for intellectual nourishment as well.

And so, in recent years, I have made reading and learning a priority in my daily life. In just the last few weeks alone, thanks to the books I've read, I have traveled to some fascinating locations around the world, including Easter Island in the South Pacific, Ayre's Rock in Australia, the Hypogeum in Malta, as well Machu Picchu in Peru and Angor Wat in Cambodia. I've also managed to spend some quality time in a quaint English village (circa early 1800s) just sixteen miles outside of London. I'm hoping to explore new territory with a swim to Antarctica alongside the amazing open-sea swimmer and memoirist Lynne Cox . . . all while being a full-time mom to my kids.

Other mothers ask me how I fit so much reading time into my days. I tell them that it's really not so hard to do. First of all, I rarely watch television because it offers little in the way of competition to the books on my nightstand. Like many moms I know, I squeeze in a little reading time each night before dropping off to sleep, but I also sneak in some reading time during the day when my toddler takes a nap and my other kids are at school or engaging in relatively quiet activities. I also make a point of carrying a book with me whenever I leave home so I can read a few pages whether I'm waiting for a doctor's appointment or for a child's violin lesson to end.

In the last few years, I've increased my reading and learning time by listening to audiobooks as well as taped lectures by college professors (some wonderful educational companies make such lectures available for purchase). I find time to listen to such books and lectures when I'm walking our family dog, running errands around town, or doing household chores after the kids are in bed. For instance, on those evenings when I feel I can no longer put off mopping my floors, I find consolation in the company of author Emily Watts as she shares her reverent yet humorous take on family life through the audio version of her book, *Being the Mom*. By the end of such an evening, my floors shine, but even better, I feel like I've enjoyed the evening in the company of a wise, engaging, and reassuring mothering friend.

I enjoy reading and learning on my own, but I also enjoy sharing my love for reading and learning with my kids. Together, we read everything from beloved picture books to some especially engaging educational magazines. We also enjoy reading aloud from fictional chapter books as well as biographies on individuals like Helen Keller or Wilbur and Orville Wright. Such stories inspire my children to become more aware of their talents and to set goals for themselves and then to work hard to achieve those goals. It is my hope that our shared learning experiences will instill in my kids the desire and permission they need to be lifelong learners. There is one thing I know for sure—we have created many fond memories through our shared reading times together.

With all of the reading and learning that takes place in our home, we strive to choose only from the best books and resources. With the advent of the Internet, it has become especially clear that information does not necessarily equal truth or goodness. With such a wealth of information now so easily available at our fingertips, we must be careful and even prayerful in our pursuit of knowledge.

When I'm making selections for reading or study, I find it helpful to keep in mind the thirteenth Article of Faith, which states, in part, "If there is anything virtuous, lovely, or of good report or praiseworthy, we seek after these things." I find a few questions helpful as well: *Will this help my children and me to grow closer to Heavenly Father and his Son? Will we appreciate God's creations better after reading this? Will this help my children and me to understand and love our brothers and sisters more? Will we be better children of God because we've read or studied this?*

In this day and time, I think it is especially important to remember the scriptural admonition that to be learned is good if we will hearken unto the counsels of God (see 2 Nephi 9:29). With this counsel in mind, perhaps the most important question we can ask as we seek learning in our homes is this—*Is the gospel of Jesus Christ at the center of our learning?* In speaking of the Savior's injunction "learn of me" (Matthew 11:29), President Gordon B. Hinckley (while serving in the Quorum of the Twelve) said this: "I should like to suggest that you follow that injunction given by the Son of God. With all of your learning, learn of him. With all of your study, seek knowledge of the Master. That knowledge will complement in a wonderful way the secular training you receive and give a fullness to your life and character that can come in no other way."[1]

I understand now that the Lord truly approves of my desire as a mom to continue to seek knowledge and learning and to encourage my kids to do the same. I also realize that when it comes to seeking knowledge in this big, wide world, we and our children can go it on our own. But when I listen to the prophet and study the scriptures, it is clear to me that there is a better way. And that better way is to seek to learn of him first and then to take his counsel as we and our families seek to study and learn from the best of what this world has to offer.

Notes

1   In *Conference Report*, Oct. 1964, 118.

Chapter Ten

LIGHTING OUR CHILDREN'S JOURNEYS

> *And I know, O Lord, that thou hast all power, and can do whatsoever thou wilt for the benefit of man; therefore touch these stones, O Lord, with thy finger, and prepare them that they may shine forth in darkness; and they shall shine forth unto us in the vessels which we have prepared, that we may have light while we shall cross the sea.*
>
> —ETHER 3:4

I have always been moved by the story of the brother of Jared and his preparations for his family's journey to the promised land. I cannot help but cheer him on as he follows the Lord's instructions to build airtight barges to cross the great and sometimes turbulent waters. I want the brother of Jared to succeed in his journey, for he and his family to make it safely to the promised land.

I love the way the Lord gives the brother of Jared specific instructions for some aspects of the trip preparations but then asks him for his input when it comes to lighting the interior of the barges during the journey. Specifically, the Lord asks the brother of Jared, "What will ye that I should do that ye may have light in your vessels? For behold, ye cannot have windows, for they will be dashed in pieces;

neither shall ye take fire with you, for ye shall not go by the light of fire" (Ether 2:23).

In answer to the Lord's question, the brother of Jared climbs to the top of Mount Shelem and moltens sixteen small stones out of rock. The stones are white and clear, even transparent as glass. To me, they hardly seem the beginning of a solution to the lighting problem. Even so, the brother of Jared holds the rocks in his hands and cries unto the Lord, saying, "O Lord, thou hast given us a commandment that we must call upon thee, that from thee we may receive according to our desires" (Ether 3:2). He pleads with the Lord that his people will not have to suffer to go across the raging deep in darkness (see Ether 3:3). And then with enormous faith, the brother of Jared asks the Lord to touch the stones that they may shine forth and light the interiors of the barges. The Lord responds to the brother of Jared's great demonstration of faith by stretching forth his hand and touching the stones, one by one, with his finger. And they did have light while they traveled across the sea.

I have revisited this powerful Book of Mormon story many times over the years. Most recently, I reviewed it while preparing a lesson for a youth Sunday School class. As I prayed and pondered about how best to teach the story to my students, the Lord blessed me with specific inspiration and instruction. I wasn't surprised. The Lord has always blessed me with help in preparing Sunday School lessons when I have earnestly sought his help through the Spirit. What surprised me, though, was the unexpected additional inspiration I received through the Spirit. The Lord opened the eyes of my understanding, and I saw for the first time that the story of the brother of Jared contained some wonderful inspiration and instruction for me as a mother to my children.

In terms of motherhood, the first thing that struck me in this story was that the brother of Jared was being directed by the Lord to help his people cross what were sure to be some treacherous waters. As a mother, I feel like I too have been charged with the responsibility of giving my loved ones (specifically, my children) the safest passage possible through some inevitably treacherous waters. I want to do my part to get my children safely to adulthood, but I cannot help but fret and worry sometimes with all of the negative and confusing influences so prevalent in our world today. Like the brother of Jared, I find myself wanting to plead with the Lord (regarding my children),

"Suffer not that they shall go forth across this raging deep in darkness" (Ether 3:3).

I feel in a sense that the Lord has asked me in return, "What would ye have me do to light their way?" In answer to this question, I initially think of things like, "Please help them to have good Sunday School teachers. Help them to have good Seminary teachers too. And help them to choose good friends." These are all good things, and yet I have little control over them. I then recall the brother of Jared's simple solution for seeking light for the safe passage of his loved ones and remind myself that the answer to lighting my children's passage may be simpler than I think. And then I understand as I haven't understood before that if I go to the Lord in faith and ask for his help, he will make me as an instrument in his hands to light my children's journey through this troubled and sometimes very dark world.

The power of this inspiration is further intensified when I recall the scriptural counsel to "let your light so shine before men, that they may see your good works, and glorify your Father which is in Heaven" (Matthew 5:16). What better place to let our lights shine than in our own homes where we have a compelling opportunity to make a powerful impact on our children's lives? And what better light to shine in our children's lives than a light that will invite them to glorify their Father in Heaven?

So, when I think of the story of the brother of Jared and liken his story to my life as a mother, I want to make a request of the Lord similar to the one the brother of Jared made when he presented the stones to the Lord. I want to go to the Lord and pray unto him, crying out, *And I know, O Lord, that thou hast all power, and can do whatsoever thou wilt for the benefit of my children; therefore touch my spirit, touch my life O Lord, with thy finger and prepare me that I may shine forth in the darkness of my children's lives that they shall have light while we shall cross the sea of this life together* (adapted from Ether 3:4). Yes, this is the prayer I carry in my heart while raising children in these latter days.

To be light-givers in our children's lives, we must exercise faith in the Lord and ask him to touch our lives, to fill us with light so that we can, in turn, share that light with our children. This does not happen as a one-time event. Rather, it is an ongoing process, a process in which we must be sure to do our part to keep our lights charged and vibrant.

I am moved to action when I read the scripture, "The light of the body is the eye: if therefore thine eye be single, thy whole body shall be full of light" (Matthew 6:22). This scripture serves as a reminder to me that we must be wholehearted, focused, and disciplined in our efforts to nourish ourselves in the gospel on a regular, even daily, basis if we are to have the light we desire to shine in our children's lives. There is not time or space to become distracted by things that are unimportant in the eternal scheme of things. There is too much at stake. Neither do we have the luxury of becoming filled with doubts about our abilities as mothers. Our children need all the power and light that we can, with the Lord's help, provide in fulfilling our sacred callings as their mothers. We must do our part on a daily basis to fill ourselves with the light of the gospel (through our feasting upon the scriptures, meditation, prayers, and so forth) so we can then fill our children's lives with gospel light.

There is a part of me that wishes for smooth sailing in my children's lives rather than the sometimes rough ride caused by the turbulent waters so prevalent in our world today. I try to remind myself that smooth sailing would teach our children and us little or nothing in this life. I also keep in mind the scripture that contains an important spiritual truth: "For it must needs be that there is an opposition in all things" (2 Nephi 2:11). While the Lord's plan allows for our children to experience opposition, to ride through what sometimes feels like the raging deep, he does not require that they ride in darkness. Rather, we as parents can help to light our children's journeys if we will consistently nourish ourselves in gospel light.

It is important to remember that our children's journeys do not end once they are grown. In fact, in some ways, their journeys are just beginning when they leave our homes. And no doubt, they will need as much light as possible when they venture out on their own. If we will strive to be light-givers to our children while they are in our care and work to teach them to seek light themselves from the true source of all light, we will be giving them the best possible shot at making safe passage through this life. And, as we do our part to teach our children to seek for light themselves, we will find comfort in knowing that they need never ride in darkness, no matter how turbulent the waters of their journeys may become.

Chapter Eleven

PRAYING UNTO THE LORD FOR THE CONSECRATION OF OUR WORK

> *But behold, I say unto you that ye must pray always, and not faint; that ye must not perform any thing unto the Lord save in the first place ye shall pray unto the Father in the name of Christ, that he will consecrate thy performance unto thee, that thy performance may be for the welfare of thy soul.*
>
> —2 NEPHI 32:9

I must have been seven or eight years into motherhood when this scripture first struck me with its implications on the work of raising children. You and I, as mothers to our children, are doing the work of the Lord on a daily basis. He does not want us to do his work alone, so we are blessed with the scriptural reminder "that ye must not perform any thing unto the Lord save in the first place ye shall pray unto the Father in the name of Christ" (2 Nephi 32:9).

As a mother, I have taken this scripture as an invitation to go to the Lord in prayer each morning before my children wake up. During these prayers, I ask the Lord to be with me as I care for my children during the coming day. My prayers may not always be long, but they are heartfelt and help me to tune into the Spirit before I am swept along into the current of a given day.

When I begin my day with prayer, I create a calm, peaceful center from which to mother that day. I also tap into the power of the Lord's promise to consecrate my performance, that my performance may be for the welfare of my soul. *Consecrate* means to "make or declare sacred."[1] And that is exactly what I have felt—that through my prayers, the Lord has helped me to more fully recognize and live in accordance with the sacred nature of my role as a mother. I also feel that the Lord, through his consecration of my work as a mother, has helped to improve the welfare of my soul. In other words, he has helped me to become more of who he would have me be and to experience greater joy and peace in the process.

Motherhood, in and of itself, is a powerful invitation to change as an individual and to improve ourselves for the sake of our children. But, it is my experience that motherhood, in concert with the Spirit, has the potential to change us in far more powerful ways than we could ever otherwise do on our own. I am not the same woman as I was before I had children—thanks, in great part, to prayer. One of my younger sisters has, at times, noted how much I have changed in the years since I became a mother. I remember well the time she said, "You have become a nicer person overall since you became a mom."

I was humbled by her assessment, but I also recognize that she shared her thoughts as a compliment. And, I also know that she was right in what she said. In my defense, I do not think my sister would say that I was mean or cruel before I had kids, but, looking back, even I can see that I was self-centered and overly focused on what I needed and wanted without much regard to others' wants or needs. Motherhood, accompanied with an abundance of prayer, has softened my heart and helped me to become more sensitive to the needs of others and more determined and resourceful in meeting those needs.

I have found that parenthood, accompanied by prayers, has changed me in other ways as well. I am more thoughtful and more focused in my priorities now. Before I had children, I generally found ways to cram everything in that I wanted to do in a given day or week. Now, in the heat of raising a family, I find it impossible to get everything done, ever. And so, I make more conscious, prayerful choices about what I want to do in a given day or in a given week. In effect, prayerful motherhood has helped me to focus on what's really important (like having daily family prayer) and to worry less about what's not as important (like having a perfectly tidy house before I go to bed at night).

Perhaps the biggest change in who I am since I became a parent, and especially a parent who prays, is that I am more teachable than I used to be. There was a time when I thought I had all the answers to raising kids—and then I had kids of my own. And, I have been humbled. Parenthood has brought me face to face with my weaknesses and inadequacies in ways that I don't think any other experience could have done. With the help of prayer, I am more willing now to look at my weaknesses and to work to change them.

And as a prayerful parent, I have become more selective in who I seek as my teachers. As I have gone to the Lord, I have become far more aware of the relevance of the Savior's example to parenthood. In his lifetime, the Savior displayed the patience, focus, and compassion that I want so much to possess as a mother. So, I seek to learn of him and from him so I can become more like him. To this end, I study the scriptures with an eye to learning more about his earthly ministry and the eternal truths he taught while here.

In my efforts to learn from inspired, righteous teachers, I seek to absorb more fully the inspired words and counsel of Church leaders, particularly through general conference talks. I have never listened to or read from a conference talk without finding something that I can apply in my role as a parent.

I also seek to be taught directly by the Spirit. For, as the scriptures say, "I say unto you that if ye will enter in by the way, and receive the Holy Ghost, it will show unto you all things what ye should do" (2 Nephi 32:5).

So, in striving to be prayerful and teachable, I have been blessed as a mother with a better perspective and better answers than I could ever find on my own. In seeking to be taught by the best teachers— the Savior, inspired Church leaders, and the Holy Ghost, I feel I am making progress toward becoming the best teacher I can possibly be for my kids.

While I feel I am making progress in becoming the person the Lord wants me to be, I realize that I still have a long way to go. So, I keep rowing my boat, I keep making my way along this earthly path on the relatively smooth days as well as on the tough days. As I make my way, I never cease to be amazed at how much the work of raising our children can challenge us. Given my years of experience, the many prayers I have poured out to heaven over the years, and the lessons I have learned as a parent, I sometimes expect that parenting should be getting much easier by now. And yet, I continue to be challenged every day as I work to raise my children.

These thoughts tugged at the back of my mind when my husband and I came across some unexpected quiet time to talk early one morning. We used this time to discuss our current parenting struggles before our kids awakened. Among other things, we talked about our fifteen-year-old, who thought she was plenty old enough to be completely in charge of herself; our nine-year-old, who wanted to be in charge of everyone else in the family whether they liked it or not; and our two-year-old, who didn't want to be in charge of anyone but wanted to be allowed to get into everything he could get his hands on, whether it was the vitamins hidden on top of the fridge or my secret chocolate stash that apparently wasn't so secret after all.

As my husband and I shared our frustrations and mulled over possible solutions for our various parenting challenges, I couldn't help but blurt out, "Why does parenting have to be so hard?" A couple of thoughts immediately came to mind, including something about children having wills of their own and the fact that anything truly worthwhile usually takes a significant amount of work and sacrifice. But, another answer came to mind as well—the answer that parenting might be hard, in part, because as we raise our children, we are working our way toward our own salvation. And it makes no sense to me that our salvation should come easily. After all, something that comes easily isn't going to help us to learn or grow. And besides, what value would an easy salvation hold?

I find it helpful to remember that we are not alone in raising our children or in working our way toward our own salvation. The Lord is mindful of us. Even as we work and struggle to raise our children with their best interests at heart, the Lord has our best interests at heart. As we pray to the Lord in our role as parents, he will consecrate our performance as parents that our performance may be for the welfare of our children but also for the welfare of our own souls, and not just for the earthly welfare of our souls (as in I am kinder to my kids now, so I feel more at peace with myself because I am kinder) but for the eternal welfare of our souls as well (in that we can become more like the Savior and move closer to perfection and our own salvation as we go along).

As we make our way through our day-to-day lives, let us find comfort in knowing that while we are in the trenches of parenthood, giving
our children everything we've got, the Lord is with us, giving us more
than we sometimes realize. If we will seek him through prayer, he will,
through his consecration of our work, help us to not only become the
parent our children need, but also to improve the welfare of our souls
and so lead us steadily along the path toward eternal life.

Notes

1   *Webster's New World Dictionary*, student edition (New York: Simon &
     Schuster, 1983), 202.

Chapter Twelve

FOSTERING AN ATMOSPHERE OF PEACE AND HARMONY AT HOME

> *And ye will not have a mind to injure one*
> *another, but to live peaceably, and to render to*
> *every man according to that which is his due.*
> —MOSIAH 4:13

I would like to report that all is peace and sunshine at our house, but the truth is that we have some work to do before I can accurately report such a state. With a strong desire to focus on the positive in writing about creating a more peaceful home, I recently invited my husband and children to the kitchen table and asked for their input in how we could get along better as a family.

My oldest daughter pitched in first with the suggestion that we should give each other more hugs because it's hard to fight with someone when you're hugging them. I had to agree. Then, my eleven-year-old piped in with our old family motto, "Hugs, Not Hits," and suggested that we should add, "Kisses, Not Kicks." A good idea, I thought. My nine-year-old daughter laughed her way through these suggestions, reminding me that, as a family, we need to find ways to laugh together more often and to lighten up when things get tense. My six-year-old enthusiastically added that when someone wants to fight with you, you should just say, "Peace." I appreciated her suggestion because it got right to the heart of what we wanted to invite into our home—greater peace. I suspect that all of our kids felt, on some level, that they had more than met their quota for conflicts and skirmishes in recent weeks. I think that they were each more than ready to get along better with their siblings.

My husband, seeming to note this change in tone as well, counseled our children to show more respect for each other. And, my eleven-year-old added that, as a show of respect, she and her sisters needed to work on forgiving and forgetting instead of bringing up the same old complaints about each other. I was impressed with their suggestions. Inspired by their input, I reminded them of something I used to say to them fairly regularly: "Remember that when we're with each other, we're in the best of company; so, let's act like it!"

I firmly believe that when we are with our family members we can think of ourselves as being in the best of company. And when we are in the best of company, we should not have a mind to injure one another but to live peaceably and to render unto every family member according to that which is their due (see Mosiah 4:13).

In the context of creating a peaceful home, I find myself pondering the thought, *what is due to each family member in our home?* I like to think that each family member is due a safe place in which to dwell—a place in which they feel safe physically, emotionally, and spiritually. And a place where each person wants to be present because they know they are deeply valued, loved, and respected.

My husband and I have fasted and prayed many times over our desire to create a home that feels more like a heaven on earth. Through our prayers and fasting, we have consistently received inspiration to help us along the path to increased peace in our home. One especially powerful prompting we received not long ago was to read the Book of Mormon as a family. We had certainly read and studied portions of the Book of Mormon together, but we had yet to tackle the book from cover to cover as a family. Any reservations I felt about reading the entire Book of Mormon as a family were replaced with enthusiasm and eagerness when I discovered this powerful quote by Marion G.

Romney, former second counselor in the First Presidency:

> I feel certain that if, in our homes, parents will read from the Book of Mormon prayerfully and regularly, both by themselves and with their children, the spirit of that great book will come to permeate our homes and all who dwell therein. The spirit of reverence will increase; mutual respect and consideration for each other will grow. The spirit of contention will depart. Parents will counsel their children in greater love and wisdom. Children will be more responsive and submissive to the counsel of their parents. Righteousness will increase. Faith, hope and charity—the pure love of Christ—will abound in our homes and lives, bringing in their wake peace, joy and happiness.[1]

What a powerful challenge and promise! When I read this quote again months later, I realized that our family had fallen down in our efforts to consistently read and study the Book of Mormon together. And that is what we need to get back to. We can brainstorm forever over possible solutions to increasing the level of peace in our home. But, until we nourish ourselves with the scriptures, individually and as a family, we are only scratching at the surface of creating a peaceful and happy home.

In my experience, when we undertake an active study of the scriptures in our homes, we will naturally want to take other positive actions as well, actions that invite even greater peace into our homes. When our scripture study is in place, we will be inclined to pray more focused, meaningful prayers. This should be no surprise when we recognize that a focused study of the scriptures does much to tutor us in the language of the Spirit. And when we are tutored in the language of the Spirit, we will feel a deeper desire to communicate with the Lord on a daily basis. And such communication, in and of itself, does much to invite greater calm into our homes.

My husband and I have also found that regular communication with the Lord, through the Spirit, blesses us with more powerful and plentiful inspiration in how we can invite greater peace into our home. Over the years, I have received specific promptings in many areas that have helped to increase the peace in our home. Among them, I have felt impressed, at times, to make sure that my children and I are getting enough rest. Heeding this prompting alone has helped to increase the peace in our home since fatigue makes even the mildest-mannered family member grumpy. At other times, I have received promptings to watch a particular child's diet. When I have done so, I have found that a lack of balance in diet has resulted in an imbalance in mood.

On many occasions I have felt impressed to use music as a way of positively influencing the mood in our home. I have found that few things can calm the atmosphere of home as beautifully as a soothing CD playing softly in the background. Our family seems especially calmed by the Mormon Tabernacle Choir's *Consider the Lilies* or *Peace Like a River* CDs and the comforting and inspiring violin music of Jenny Oaks Baker.

These days, I am seeking answers in how to encourage each of my kids to take more ownership in improving their relationships with their siblings. I want to find ways to teach each of them to take fuller responsibility for their actions in their relationships rather than automatically resorting to a mode of blaming their siblings for any discord. I want to better teach my kids the skills they need to work their way through disagreements with their siblings without hurting each other. And, I want to teach them to more actively value one another with their words and through their actions.

Finding specific answers and methods to address these issues may take the whole of my mothering life. However, if my husband and I raise our children in the context of the gospel, we are more likely to experience joy and peace in the process. And the good news of the gospel is that my husband and I are not alone in teaching our children. We can help our children to take steps that will allow them to be taught by the Spirit as well.

Looking back, I can see that when our family actively feasts upon the scriptures, our children are more inclined to soak in and share the calming influence of the Spirit. At times such as this, we also find that our children are more open to receiving and heeding specific promptings and inspiration. Our children have touched our hearts more than a few times when they have received and acted upon spiritual promptings themselves.

One such time occurred when one of my daughters, eight years old at the time, took some inspired action to transform what had been a deeply disappointing day for her into a positive and uplifting day for the entire family. We had recently moved to a new city, and my daughter felt down because she didn't have any friends to play with yet. Her sisters, for whatever reason, had chosen to give her an especially hard time that day.

Instead of retaliating, my daughter came to me, seeking a listening ear and some comfort. At eight-months-plus pregnant with my fifth child, I was too exhausted to single-handedly transform the day, but I wanted to do what I could to help. So, we made ourselves comfortable in a couple of lawn chairs on the front porch where my daughter talked and I listened. After just a few minutes of talking, my daughter began to smile. She appeared to be harboring a wonderful secret—one she preferred not to share. Instead of saying anything more, she asked to be excused and walked into the house.

Some time later, I got up and walked into the house as well. As soon as I opened the front door, I spotted a hot-pink slip of paper stuck to the coat closet door. Someone had written a message on it. It read, "You are the #1 Mom!" Looking to the left, I saw another note stuck to the wall that said, "You sure know how to make me feel better." More notes paved the path to my bedroom where I discovered my daughter making my bed and straightening my room. She beamed as I gave her a big hug and thanked her.

She didn't stop there. Instead, she busied herself creating more love-note stickies and posting them around the bedroom for her dad. By now her sisters had discovered what she was doing and joined in by performing their own kind deeds. What started out as one inspired choice on my daughter's part—to take a bad day and turn it into a good day with simple but loving acts of service for others—caught on. She showed us, through her example, that one family member moved by the Spirit can help to change the atmosphere of home and family in some much-needed and wonderful ways.

My husband and I have renewed our efforts to read and study from the Book of Mormon as a family on a daily basis as well. And not surprisingly, in just a few days, we felt the truth of President Romney's words when he said, "I feel certain that if, in our homes, parents will read from the Book of Mormon prayerfully and regularly, both by themselves and with their children, the spirit of that great book will come to permeate our homes and all who dwell therein." And not surprisingly, just as President Romney promised, we have found that "the pure love of Christ . . . will abound in our homes and lives, bringing in their wake peace, joy, and happiness" when we immerse ourselves and our families in the Book of Mormon.

With President Romney's promise in mind, my husband and I plan to make some small but important changes to our family's future discussions on getting along. We will continue to invite our children to make their own suggestions for how we can all get along better with each other. But before we invite our kids to share their ideas, we will open our discussion with a word of prayer and then ask ourselves as a family a simple but powerful question—*Have we read from the Book of Mormon today?* And, if the answer is *No*, we will know exactly where we need to begin if we want to invite peace and harmony into our home and family life.

Notes

1   "The Book of Mormon," *Ensign*, May 1980, 67.

Chapter Thirteen

TEACHING OUR CHILDREN TO KEEP THE COMMANDMENTS

> *O remember, my son, and learn wisdom in thy youth; yea, learn in thy youth to keep the commandments of God.*
>
> —ALMA 37:35

We live in a world where sin is increasingly glamorized and God's laws are mocked more and more all the time. Even so, I want very much to raise children who choose to live God's commandments. After all, I agree wholeheartedly with the children's Primary song that exclaims, "Keep the commandments! In this there is safety; in this there is peace."[1] As much as possible, I want my children to know peace and to live in safety.

Noting the tone of our times, I have pondered a great deal over how best to teach my children the importance of keeping the commandments and how best to help them understand the power that comes from doing so. Through inspiration, I have come up with an analogy that I like to share with my kids. The analogy goes something like this:

Suppose that you were dropped into a vast wilderness thousands of miles away from anything familiar to you and then told to find your way home. Would you accept help in the form of a guidebook to tell you what paths to take, what pitfalls and dangers to avoid? Would you allow someone to give you a map to use that marks the safest, most reliable route home? Or would you balk at any such offers of help, calling them too restrictive of your freedom to find your own way home?

When I have shared this scenario with my kids and asked them what they would do in such circumstances, they've sometimes joked and said, "Oh sure Mom, I'd try to find my way home on my own without any help at all." But they and I know that if they were really faced with such circumstances, they would accept whatever help necessary to find their way back home.

I tell my kids that our earthly journey is, in some ways, like a journey through a wilderness—a spiritual wilderness, to be sure. I remind them that our Heavenly Father sent us to earth to learn and to grow but he also invited us to find our way back to him. Being the loving Father that he is, he has not asked us to find our way home alone. Rather, he has given us the scriptures, the prophets, and other Church leaders to teach us about keeping the commandments that will lead us back to him. I tell my kids that keeping God's commandments helps us to avoid spiritual and even mortal danger on our journey through this earthly wilderness and that keeping the commandments helps us to stay on the sure path back to him and to find joy in our earthly journey.

While I find this analogy helpful in teaching my children the importance of keeping the commandments, sharing such an analogy is only a beginning. There is so much more that we as parents can do to teach our children about keeping the commandments. First of all, we must be sure to familiarize our children with the commandments; if we do not take this responsibility seriously, I believe that the sin will be upon our heads. So, we must make a point of educating our children in God's commandments—from the Ten Commandments to the Word of Wisdom. Some of our teaching will occur naturally during the daily course of our lives, but we should also make it a point to carve out time in our lives with the specific intention of teaching our children the commandments. Family home evening alone provides an excellent opportunity for doing this.

It seems to me that the most compelling way to teach our children to keep the commandments is to keep them ourselves. I know from my own experience, as a kid and as a mom, that our children will generally listen to what we have to say, but even more they will watch closely to see what our actions are saying. With this thought in mind, I sometimes pause to ask myself, "What are my actions saying to my children about keeping the commandments?" I hope and pray that my actions are letting them know that I am committed to keeping the commandments of God whether those commandments are to honor my own father and mother or to keep the Sabbath day holy. I hope that my actions do not give my children any rationalization for not keeping the commandments themselves.

There is a wonderful Book of Mormon scripture that makes me ponder further the kind of example I am setting for my kids when it comes to keeping the commandments. In this scripture, King Benjamin addresses his people, saying, "And moreover, I would desire that ye should consider on the blessed and happy state of those that keep the commandments of God" (Mosiah 2:41). When my children look at me, do they see a mother who feels blessed in keeping the commandments? Do they see a mom who radiates happiness as she strives to live in sync with the Lord's laws?

I would like to answer with a wholehearted yes, and, in many respects, I can do just that. But, as earnest as my efforts are overall, I am aware that there is room for improvement in some areas. For example, in my efforts to keep the Sabbath day holy, I would like to take steps to make the day happier and more enjoyable. Like most moms I know, I work hard all week long taking care of my family, striving to meet their needs for food, guidance, and nurturance. I am glad to do this, and yet I confess that by most Saturday nights I am so exhausted and ready to collapse that I sometimes end up collapsing into Sundays without being prepared for them.

With the desire to experience more pleasant Sabbath days in my home, I am working to make some positive changes in how my family gets ready for Sundays. Whenever possible, I now try to prepare our Sunday meals earlier in the week, perhaps by making a double batch of spaghetti sauce on Tuesday and freezing half for Sunday. I am also in the process of making some Sabbath day checklists for my children to complete (with help, if necessary) by suppertime on Saturdays. Their lists include laying their (clean) Sunday clothes and shoes out, preparing Primary talks if needed, and having their scriptures set out and ready to go to church.

With my kids' help, I am creating a "Sunday Can-Do" list to post on the fridge that highlights individual and family activities that we can enjoy on the Sabbath day. This list keeps my kids positively focused on what they can do on the Sabbath day rather than leaving them to dwell on the things we refrain from doing on Sundays. Collectively, these various actions—from fixing Sabbath meals earlier in the week to using our handy checklists—are helping us to keep a more joyful and more spiritually centered Sabbath day in our home. I'm thrilled to say that I'm beginning to experience the Sabbath day as the more restful, joyful day I know it was intended to be.

When my children see me as a happy mom in keeping the commandments, whether it's in keeping the Sabbath day holy or in living the Word of Wisdom (by eating a wholesome diet rather than subsisting on those tempting sweets), they are more likely to want to keep the commandments themselves.

As important as it is for us to show our children the joy that comes from keeping the commandments, we must also share with them the consequences that come from not living in accordance with the commandments. First and foremost, we should share with them what the Lord has said: "But inasmuch as ye will not keep my commandments ye shall be cut off from my presence" (2 Nephi 1:20). I feel terribly sad when I read about being cut off from the presence of the Lord. Even so, it is an important warning. After all, being cut off from the presence of the Lord, or being cut off from the guidance of the Spirit, leaves us wandering alone in the wilderness. No doubt, we want better for us and our children than to be cut off from the presence of the Lord.

Despite our best efforts, our children—as they grow older—may be dazzled by the fun the world seems to sometimes have when living out of step with the commandments. It is true that there is fun to be had in living "of the world," but let's make sure our kids know that it is the kind of fun that is shallow and, at most, temporary. My children and I have experience with loved ones and friends who have forsaken the commandments in favor of temporary fun or satisfaction. Our hearts have ached as they have ultimately experienced a loss of peace and even great sorrow over the consequences of their choices. We have, with love for these individuals, discussed with our children what we have learned from their painful experiences. I have tried to help my children see what they can do differently to stay in tune with the Spirit, to live in step with Heavenly Father's commandments.

When I think of the temptations that our youth face, I recall a Sunday School class I attended during my college years. The teacher was presenting a lesson on obeying the commandments and avoiding sin. During his lesson, he posed the question, "What can we do to avoid sin?" Some students suggested praying. Others suggested avoiding temptation and attending church meetings. As I pondered his question myself, an answer came to mind that has shaped my life ever since. I now share this answer with my children: "Choose to fill your life so full of the good things that you will have no desire or time to sin." To me, this means filling our lives with positive, uplifting activities such as developing our talents, spending time with friends who are fun and who make good choices, and finding meaningful ways in which to serve others—so much so that sin seems uninviting and unrewarding in comparison. I tell my kids that the commandments can serve as the ultimate guide to filling our lives with what is good and can bring us happiness by helping us avoid that which would harm us and others.

It is no small task to teach our children in this day and time to live the commandments of God. But it is important to do so. If we will do our part to teach our children to keep the commandments while they are in their youth, if we will show them the way through our examples, we will spare them great heartache and give them an invaluable service. For, by teaching our children to keep the commandments of God, we will show them how to find their way through the wilderness of this earthly life and back to their Father in Heaven.

Notes

1   "Keep the Commandments," *Children's Songbook* (Salt Lake City: The Church of Jesus Christ of Latter-day Saints, 1989), 148.

Chapter Fourteen

HELPING OUR CHILDREN TO FIND PEACE IN TROUBLED TIMES

> *And all thy children shall be taught of the Lord;*
> *and great shall be the peace of thy children.*
> —3 NEPHI 22:13

One of my goals as a mother is to raise children who possess a deep sense of inner peace, even in the midst of what seems to be increasingly turbulent times. Seeking to achieve this goal is proving to be no small task in a world that seems awash in violence and turmoil. We have all witnessed, through television or in person, the chaos and human suffering that can be caused by natural disasters. We have also sadly seen the pain and loss of life that can be caused by man's inhumanity to man through cruel acts of violence.

We know that at least some of these events, as painful as they can be to witness, are a fulfillment of the prophecies leading up to the Savior's Second Coming. Even knowing this, we can, if we are not careful, become consumed with fear and worry over what is going on in our world today, so much so that we lose any sense of peace and hope for our children and their future. And when this happens, we can deepen our children's own worries and fears without intending to. But this does not have to happen. There is a better way to raise our children in these latter days. And that better way is to seek peace for ourselves and to become ever more conscious of nurturing peace in our children even as we face troubling times.

How do we nurture this sense of peace in our children in a world and time such as ours? I remember well the time I carried this question in my heart as I searched the Book of Mormon, looking for answers. When I read through 3 Nephi 22:13, I knew that I had found the answer I was looking for, the answer I needed to hear. Referring to the last days, the passage reads, "And all thy children shall be taught of the Lord; and great shall be the peace of thy children." This passage helps me as a mother because it gives me clear instructions: to teach my children of the Lord. And it comforts me because it gives me a specific promise of something wonderful that will happen if I follow the inspired instructions: great shall be the peace of my children.

In studying the scriptures, it is clear to me that Jesus Christ is the Lord of Peace. If we want to nurture a strong sense of inner peace in our children, one that will persist even in difficult times, we must help our children come to know the Savior through his teachings, his example, and his promises. There is no better way to do this than to immerse our children in the scriptural accounts of the Savior's life and his teachings during his time on earth. The scriptures are filled with accounts of Christ sharing peace with others during his earthly sojourn. We can help our children feel this peace when we share with them the Savior's Sermon on the Mount (see Matthew 5–7) and tell them of his invitations to the little ones to come unto him to be blessed even as he ministered to the multitudes (see 3 Nephi 17:21).

I find that the account of Jesus in a boat on the Sea of Galilee with his disciples serves as an especially powerful reminder to us and our children of the peace the Savior can bring into our lives if we will seek his help. In this account, Jesus had fallen asleep and a great storm arose. The winds blew very hard and the waves beat into the boat (see Mark 4:37). The disciples were afraid. They awoke Jesus and asked him to help. Jesus "rebuked the wind and said unto the sea, Peace be still. And the wind ceased and there was a great calm" (Mark 4:39). I tell my children that just as the Savior calmed the storm on the Sea of Galilee, he can, if we seek his help in faith, calm our troubled hearts in difficult times.

In our home, my husband and I also strive to help our children understand the peace the Savior offers through his teachings on keeping the commandments, being prepared, loving and serving others, forgiving those who have done us or others wrong, and so forth. We spend many family home evenings focused on the Savior's teachings. One night we talk about the importance of being prepared (the story of the Ten Virgins serves well on this night) and on another night we talk about loving, serving, and finding peace in good times and in difficult times by following the Savior's example and loving and serving our brothers and sisters.

We try to instill in our children the importance of living righteously if they want to experience peace in this world. We support our teaching by sharing scriptures such as this: "But learn that he who doeth the works of righteousness shall receive his reward, even peace in this world, and eternal life in the world to come" (D&C 59:23). In great part, we tell our children, this peace comes because as we live righteously we are entitled to receive the promptings, inspiration, and comfort of the Holy Ghost. And it is through the Holy Ghost that the Savior sends his peace.

If we want our children to feel and know peace in this life, we must, above all, be sure to teach them about the atoning sacrifice of the Savior, Jesus Christ. And how, because of his great sacrifice, we can know that this life will continue beyond the veil of death, that thanks to the Savior's sacrifice we can, even when we witness tragedy or experience tragedy firsthand, know that this life is but a step in our Heavenly Father's great plan of happiness.

As parents, we must be sure to do our part to help our children understand and gain their own testimonies of these truths. We can nurture and strengthen our children's testimonies by sharing the words of Jesus himself. I am especially moved by the calming words the Savior spoke to his disciples shortly before his death: "Let not your heart be troubled: ye believe in God, believe also in me. In my Father's house are many mansions: if it were not so, I would have told you. I go to prepare a place for you. . . . that where I am, there ye may be also. . . . Peace I leave with you, my peace I give unto you: not as the world giveth, give I unto you. Let not your heart be troubled, neither let it be afraid" (John 14:1–3, 27). We can teach our children that when we look to the Savior, our fear is replaced with feelings of power and love and the experience of a sound mind (see 2 Timothy 1:7), the very qualities that will bring us peace and help us to know how best to navigate troubling times.

Two things have become increasingly clear to me as I have sought to help my children find peace in these latter days:

First, the peace that is available to us through Jesus Christ does not make us immune to experiencing tough times. After all, we know that this life is a test and that there must needs be opposition in all things (see 2 Nephi 2:11). In the words of LDS author George S. Tate, "This peace is of a special kind. It gives no assurance against hardship; the apostles [who served with Jesus] suffered all kinds of trials and finally death by martyrdom." He adds that the Savior himself has said, " '*In me* ye might have peace. In the world ye shall have tribulation' (John 16:33)."[1] So, the peace the Savior gives is not a matter of external events, but rather it is determined by our inner relationship with the Lord.

The second thing that has become especially clear to me is that if we want our children to posses peace in this world, we must make sure that we posses such peace ourselves. After all, our children will generally take their cues from us. So, if necessary, let us increase our own understanding of the Savior's teachings while he was on the earth. Let us strengthen our testimonies of Heavenly Father's great plan of happiness and the Savior's part in that plan through the Atonement. Let us be sure to live our lives in a way that helps us to be open and attentive to the comforting inspiration and promptings of the Spirit.

My husband and I have found the promptings and inspiration of the Spirit to be invaluable in helping us support and comfort our children in times of crisis and tragedy, whether those crises or tragedies are witnessed through the media or felt closer to home. Of course, we have consistently felt prompted to share our understanding of the Savior with our children. But we have felt prompted in other ways as well. For example, we have felt prompted to filter carefully the news that our children hear and see through the various media outlets. We have come to believe that if we allow our children unfiltered access to the news, they will be left with the false impression that they are in imminent danger just walking out the front door of our home on any given day. And we see no reason to undermine our children's sense of peace in such a way.

At other times in response to a disaster or tragedy, we have felt prompted to help our children find ways in which they can make a difference for those who have been injured or who have lost their loved ones. We tell them that this is what Jesus would do. And our children have felt great peace and healing when they have helped those in need by earning money to donate to relief efforts or by writing letters of cheer and comfort to the victims of a tragedy.

One of the most powerful bits of inspiration we have received is to take time to really listen to our kids as they discuss their worries and concerns about a troubling event or the threat of a troubling event. We cannot do our part to help our children find peace if we do not have a good grasp of their feelings and thoughts.

My husband and I have had many opportunities to put to work what we have learned about instilling peace in our children. The most poignant time in recent history for us was when two families we knew and loved were the victims of devastating but unrelated house fires in the same week. The cause of the first house fire was never conclusively determined but appeared to have been caused by a childish prank done by someone outside the family, a prank that went terribly awry. Sadly, the entire family lost their lives—a mother, a father, their three teenaged children, and a friend who had been spending the night. The second house fire occurred just six days later and was caused by a middle-of-the night lightning strike on my older sister's house. My sister, her husband, and their six children woke to find their house on fire. They managed to escape unharmed but lost their home and almost all of their material possessions.

Our children were terribly upset by these two events, especially given that they occurred in such rapid succession. During this period, my husband and I spent a great deal of time in prayer determining how best to help our children process these events. We also prayed a great deal as a family. We reviewed the plan of salvation with our children and shared our testimonies of life after this life. We also talked about the importance of preparation in the event of a fire in our own home. We spent a family night checking our smoke detectors and installing additional smoke detectors. We developed a clearer plan for escaping in the event of a house fire and practiced fire drills. We shared with each other what we loved about the friends we had lost in the first fire, expressed gratitude for having known them, and shared our desires to follow their positive examples in how we live our own lives. We also helped to start a relief fund for my sister's family and to send them gifts that would help and comfort them as they rebuilt their lives.

In helping our children to process these sad and sobering events, we found it especially important to spend extra time with them, letting them express their fears and feelings of loss while we listened. Some of our discussions occurred in family settings, and others occurred spontaneously in the car or as we tucked our children into bed at night. As we listened to our children and tuned in to the Spirit, we found ourselves better equipped than we otherwise would have been to address their fears and questions and to provide them with the peace and assurance they stood in need of.

During this time, our sense of peace as a family was shaken. Our hearts ached. We were filled with grief. But, together, we learned again what we had already known—that we can find comfort in our knowledge of the gospel of Jesus Christ. When we are faced with troubling times, we and our children can tap into an unfailing source of peace, a peace that only the Savior can give—a peace that can bring comfort, healing, assurance, and direction even in the darkest of times.

Notes

1   "The Peace of Christ," *Ensign*, Apr. 1978, 46.

Chapter Fifteen

SUPPORTING EACH OTHER
AS MOTHERS

> *And he commanded them . . . that they should look forward with one eye, having one faith and one baptism, having their hearts knit together in unity and in love one towards another.*
> —MOSIAH 18:21

Some years ago, I attended a ward with a sister who greatly impressed me with her earnest efforts to be a good mother to her four children. She did many things right in parenting her kids—from striving to hold family home evening each week to teaching her kids how to prepare wholesome and tasty meals on a budget. And, she served her children in an amazing variety of ways on a daily basis and worked to raise them in an atmosphere of love. I noticed that she was sometimes especially hard on herself when she made mistakes in parenting her kids, but I think even she knew that overall she was doing a good job as a parent.

What intrigued me so much about this mother was that she was striving to raise her own children with far more love and care than she

had ever experienced in her own childhood. She has never shared much
about her upbringing with me, but from the little bit I have gleaned
over the years, there was enough emotional and physical abuse and
neglect to break almost any mother's heart.

Given what I know of this sister's background, I have long wondered how she ever learned to be such a good mother herself. Finally,
one day, after so many years of wondering, I simply asked her, "Where
did you learn to raise your children with so much love when you grew
up with so little?" Her face immediately softened and she smiled as she
answered, "I learned from the sisters in Relief Society."

My friend went on to share some of the many ways her Relief Society sisters had helped her to overcome her upbringing to become the
mother she wanted and needed to be to her children. She expressed
appreciation for the sisters who had taught Relief Society lessons on
family life. She said that the comments the teachers and other sisters
shared during the lessons had inspired her and given her powerful
insights into raising her own children.

She reminisced on the times when Relief Society sisters had invited
her into their homes and how she had been touched when she watched
these mothers exercise patience with their kids and tend to them with
a tenderness so unlike what she had experienced while growing up.
She spoke fondly of how several moms had mentored her by sharing
what had worked for them as parents in ways that uplifted and encouraged her rather than making her feel less than qualified.

She also talked about the sisters who had served her and her family
by providing child care when needed or a meal when she was ill. She
marveled that these sisters had rendered their service with so much
love and without any strings attached. She was so deeply affected by
these sisters' examples overall that she sought to raise her kids with
the same Christlike spirit they had shared with her.

I have sometimes wondered if these Relief Society sisters have any
real idea of the difference they made in this woman's life. Knowing this
sister as I do, I imagine that she has expressed appreciation to those
who have touched her life over the years. Even so, I doubt that they can
possibly know the full impact of their words, their examples, and their
service in helping and supporting my friend in loving and nurturing
her children as the Lord would have her do.

These sweet sisters took fully to heart the Relief Society's mission wherein we as sisters covenant to "dedicate ourselves to strengthening marriages, families, and homes."[1] I am sure that these sisters were dedicated to strengthening their own marriages, families, and homes. But, clearly, their commitment did not end in their own homes. I can only imagine that these women have positively impacted countless numbers of their sisters over the years through their thoughtful words and actions. I know with complete certainty that they made a positive and powerful impact on my friend. And, in making such an impact, they blessed not only my friend but her children and possibly many future generations of parents and children as well.

When I think of my friend's experience, I cannot help but recall the times when the sisters in the Relief Society have made a difference in my life. One of the times I remember most appreciatively is when I miscarried in the second trimester and was rushed into emergency surgery to save my life. My head spun with the unexpected loss and threat to my life. However, that difficult time was eased considerably when my visiting teachers and other sisters from church stepped in to provide child care as well as to deliver home-cooked meals, lovely bouquets of flowers, and thoughtful cards. This was only one of the many instances when I have felt supported by my sisters in the gospel.

As sisters in Zion, we each have a profound opportunity to help create a supportive community among mothers. One of the simplest but most important ways we can each be part of doing this is by actively participating in Relief Society by attending meetings on Sundays, participating in enrichment activities, and going the extra mile in the divinely inspired visiting teaching program (which I have long viewed as a time to make and nurture friendships). When we come together in these settings, we get to know one another and learn from one another. And, in getting to know one another and learn from one another, we cannot help but come to love each other.

In my experience as a Relief Society sister, I have come to believe that one of the best gifts we can give each other as we get to know each other is to respect, appreciate, and even celebrate our differences. We share one faith, but within that one faith, there is plenty of room for many kinds of moms. In my ward alone, there is an amazing variety of moms, from the soft-spoken mother of three to the loving but firm mom of eleven who enthusiastically claims to raise her kids boot-camp style.

As members of the Church, we are counseled to avoid contention with one another and to live instead in unity and harmony one with another (see Mosiah 18:21). We can each be part of making this happen with our sisters by allowing for the inevitable differences in style and methods of parenting and by recognizing that we are all likely doing our best in raising our children. An added benefit is that the more accepting we are of mothers who are different from us, the more accepting we will be of ourselves.

As we get to know, love, and accept one another, we will inevitably want to serve one another. And given our big hearts as women, we often want to do the big things to serve each other. Sometimes, we are able to do those big things to help each other (such as child care or providing meals), but other times we may find it difficult to do the bigger things because of a lack of time, a lack of money, a personal crisis we're struggling through, and so on. When this happens, we can often still do small things to support other mothers that can make a big difference. Some of those small things can include sitting by another sister during Relief Society rather than sitting alone, calling a sister during the week to check in and see how she's doing, dropping a note in the mail to celebrate a sister's birthday, or inviting a new mother to join a play group or book club.

One of the simplest but most powerful little things we can do to support other mothers is to make a habit of sharing sincere compliments with them. A compliment, thoughtfully shared, can boost almost any mother's morale; it certainly boosts mine. I remember one Sunday when I was sitting in the pew at church just before sacrament meeting began, and for a reason I cannot now recall I was feeling particularly discouraged about my performance as a mother. While I was immersed in my thoughts, a sister in the pew behind me tapped me on the shoulder and said, "I've been meaning to tell you what a terrific mother I think you are," and then she went on to share why she thought this was so. I certainly hadn't been feeling like a terrific mom right then. But, by taking the time to share a compliment, this sister had given me some perspective and lifted my spirits just when they needed lifting.

There was another time when my spirits were in particular need of a boost. My husband and I had just moved to a new city. And while I was enjoying getting to know other mothers at church meetings and gatherings, I found myself feeling rather lonely and almost completely without adult company and conversation during the weekdays. Not helping matters any was the fact that my husband was traveling a great deal on business during that time.

For a while, I allowed myself to wallow in self-pity over my situation. But, the reality was, self-pity did little to remedy my loneliness, so I decided to step out of my comfort zone and take some serious initiative to change my circumstances. I drew up a list of the sisters I had met and wanted to get to know better and began to invite them and their kids to join me and my kids for outings at the zoo, the community pool, and elsewhere. I also started a book club for sisters who, like me, loved to read and offered to teach writing workshops for enrichment activities for anyone who was interested. In very short order, I got to know some terrific moms and made some wonderful friends. I found that once I took the initiative, the other mothers were just as eager to make new friends as I was. This experience taught me that if we want to be part of a supportive network of moms, we must focus on doing our part to create that supportive network rather than simply waiting for others to make the first move.

Prayer, I have found, can do much to help facilitate our efforts to support each other. Being prayerful can help us to be more awake and aware of the needs of the sisters around us. It can help us to have the courage to step out of our comfort zones to support each other and to receive support in return. Prayer can also help us to know when to gently offer to help another mother and when to insist on helping her despite her reluctance to accept our help. And let's not forget, prayer can turn feelings of competitiveness into feelings of compassion and pure love as we serve each other.

When I think of the compassion and caring that can exist among mothers, I think first of my friend's story of all the Relief Society sisters who have touched her life. Her experience provides a marked contrast to much of what I have seen out in the world when it comes to supporting and encouraging mothers in their work. The world seems to pay a lot of lip service to the importance of motherhood and honoring mothers, especially around Mother's Day, but in reality, it often seems to do more to diminish and even undermine motherhood than to esteem and support motherhood. And, in my opinion, the media— through magazines and television—seems to foster conflict among mothers by attempting to keep us at odds with one another rather than fostering a sense of community with each other that could be so helpful in raising our kids.

As members of the Church, we know that our work as mothers is sacred and so worthy of support and encouragement. And, as sisters in Relief Society, we are enthusiastically invited to provide that support and encouragement for each other by dedicating ourselves to "strengthening marriages, families, and homes." If we will each prayerfully seek to do what we can to strengthen marriages, families, and homes—ours and others—we will surely nurture feelings of tenderness and sisterhood among mothers. We can never know for sure the full impact of our positive actions on another mother. Nevertheless, I have no doubt but that if we as mothers will seek to support one another, to strengthen one another, and to uplift one another, we will find that our efforts will inevitably knit our hearts as sisters in unity and in love one toward another (see Mosiah 18:21).

Notes

1   The Relief Society Declaration.

Chapter Sixteen

EMBRACING OUR SPIRITUAL GIFTS

> *And again, I exhort you, my brethren, that ye*
> *not deny the gifts of God, for they are many;*
> *and they come from the same God. And there are*
> *different ways that these gifts are administered;*
> *but it is the same God who worketh all in all;*
> *and they are given by the manifestations of the*
> *Spirit of God unto men, to profit them.*
> —MORONI 10:8

When I was a young mother, I sometimes got caught up in comparing myself to other mothers, and just between you and me, I never measured up. This shouldn't have come as a surprise to anyone since I tended to measure the worst parts of myself against the best parts of other mothers as I saw them in public, whether at church or in the community.

I imagine that if I had not stopped making such unfavorable comparisons between myself and other moms, I would be a very discouraged and perhaps even miserable mom by now. And, no doubt, my children and husband would feel the brunt of such a state. After all, how we feel about ourselves directly impacts our relationships with others, especially those in our own families. There is no getting around this fact. Between you and me, I suspect that the only one who finds satisfaction in a truly unhappy mom is Satan. After all, he probably delights in few things more than a mom who feels discouraged about herself and so shares that sense of discouragement with her family.

Thankfully, over the years, as I've immersed myself in the gospel, I have grasped more fully the concept of my individual worth and the Lord's love for me as his daughter. It is clear to me now that no two mothers are alike nor should they be. So, why waste our time comparing ourselves to other mothers when the truth is that we are each incomparable? The Spirit reminds me that each mom is precious, very precious as an individual to the Lord. And each mom has her own unique set of spiritual gifts and talents that she brings to bear in the sacred work of motherhood.

When we realize this, when we take this knowledge into our hearts and into our minds and allow it to sink deeply into our spirits, the need to compare ourselves with other mothers diminishes and perhaps, over time, even disappears altogether. I have certainly found this to be true in my case. When we let go of comparing ourselves with other moms, we are in a better position to recognize, claim, and develop our spiritual gifts for the benefit and even the delight of our families, others, and even ourselves.

My heart is touched when I read the scriptural truth that "every good gift cometh of Christ" (Moroni 10:18). When we understand where our gifts come from, how can we not accept the invitation to "Come unto Christ, and lay hold upon every good gift" (Moroni 10:30)? As we work to raise our children in these latter days, let us be sure to claim all the gifts the Lord has in wait for us. If we will do this, if we will claim our gifts and develop them, we will put ourselves in the best position possible to raise our children successfully.

When I see the mothers I know honoring their own spiritual gifts in raising their children, I am inspired to honor my own. My friend Helen has a wonderful gift in the way she speaks with such conviction when she shares her testimony of the gospel. She readily shares her testimony at church, but I know that she shares it at home as well. When I listen to her bear her testimony, my testimony is strengthened. I have no doubt but that her sons draw upon her spiritual strength as they work to develop their own strong testimonies.

My friend Becky has always shared her extraordinary gift for music with her children. When each was a newborn baby in her arms, she sang gentle, soothing lullabies that I'm sure brought immense comfort to her baby and anyone else who happened to be listening. Whenever she performs a solo at church, her children watch and listen with rapt attention along with the rest of the congregation. How can her children not be moved when they hear their mother sing "How Great Thou Art" with so much feeling and power?

As a gifted pianist, Becky also composes music and lyrics that cannot help but bring joy to the soul and even healing to the spirit. It is no wonder that her oldest son recently gave such a stirring performance as the star of his high school musical. Watching him onstage, it was clear that he was not a young man who had been pressured or cajoled into musical performance, but rather he was a young man who was raised in a home that was filled with an immense and infectious love for music.

One of my own mother's greatest gifts is her special sensitivity for those who face enormous struggles but do not have much of a support network, especially in the way of family. From the time I was a little girl, I can remember my mom helping those in need in many ways: providing a listening ear, giving sound but respectful advice, and sharing home-cooked meals. Our door was always open and no one was ever a stranger in our home. Through her example, my mom taught my sisters and me much about living with Christlike love during our formative years. She raised four daughters to adulthood, but she nurtured and cared for many others along the way.

When I see my mother and so many of my mothering friends using their gifts to bless their families and others, I feel the deep desire to become more aware of my own gifts and to make the most of them in blessing my family and others.

One way I have worked to become more aware of my gifts is by making a conscious effort to really listen to and take in the compliments of friends and family members rather than readily dismissing them. I remember one such time when a non-LDS friend, Laura, attended church with me. She sat through the youth Sunday School class that I taught and later commented that she was impressed with how I made the lesson so relevant to my students' lives. She felt that my students listened to me better than they otherwise would have because I made a point of letting them know, in very specific ways, how the lesson pertained to their lives.

I realize now that this is something that I strive to do at home— to let my children know, very specifically, how gospel teachings and gospel principles apply to their lives. I do this with the hope that this approach makes a difference in my children's grasp of the gospel and desire to live the gospel throughout their lives.

On another occasion, I gained some positive perspective on my gifts as a mother in a most unexpected way. For family home evening one Monday night, I announced an impromptu talent show where each of our kids would be given five minutes to perform for the other family members. I announced to the kids that I would record their presentation on my digital voice recorder (we didn't own a video camera) and that they would have just a few minutes to prepare. Each of my kids was delighted by the thought of being the exclusive center of the family's attention for a few minutes. They each gave fun and engaging performances—from our then four-year-old daughter who spontaneously shared an energetic and surprisingly well-rhymed poetry rap to our then thirteen-year-old daughter who gave us clear verbal directions on how to draw cartoon characters as she drew some herself.

After all the children had given their performances, we listened as a family to the audio recording and were tickled to hear the kids' performances again. While listening to the tape I was caught off guard by the mom in the recording. After each child's performance she spent a minute or two sharing specifically what she liked about their performances. Her praise was enthusiastic and encouraging without being unbelievably gushing. I remember thinking, *She sounds like a loving, supportive, and even fun mom.* It surprised me to think that that mom was me! I think that experience was, in part, a gift from God letting me know that I really do have some gifts as a mother and that I am likely making a difference in my children's lives by using them. I wish every mom could catch an outside glimpse of the good she is doing with her gifts.

I do not share these experiences to boast; rather, I share them to encourage other mothers to consider their own gifts, perhaps previously overlooked. Every mom has her own unique set of God-given gifts, some still waiting to be discovered and developed. I know that sometimes some of us get caught up in saying, "I don't have any special gifts as a mom," but this simply isn't true. After all, we are spirit children of our Father in Heaven. We have his spiritual DNA. And as such, we have inherited some of his wonderful and useful traits, and we can, if we are willing, bring the special gifts we have inherited to use in raising our children.

As we strive to become more aware of our own gifts and work to develop them, we will gain greater confidence in our roles as mothers. We will also be better able to appreciate the diversity of gifts that the women around us possess and the difference those gifts make not only in their children's lives but also in *our* children's lives.

Over the years I have grown increasingly grateful for the special traits and the wonderful gifts that other women have employed in touching my children's lives whether through Primary, the Young Women program, or simply by inviting my children into their homes to play with their children. Choosing to compare ourselves to other mothers seems so uninviting when we consider the joy that can come from celebrating and encouraging each mother's special gifts (including our own) instead.

Let us seek to follow the powerful counsel to "lay hold upon every good gift" (Moroni 10:30). If we will heed this counsel, if we will seek to discover and develop our gifts as daughters of God and as mothers to our children, we will experience greater joy in motherhood overall. And, perhaps best of all, when our children see our examples of claiming and developing our gifts, they will receive the permission and encouragement they need to claim and make the most of their gifts too.

Chapter Seventeen

SPEAKING
WITH THE TONGUE
OF ANGELS

> *Do ye not remember that I said unto you that*
> *after ye had received the Holy Ghost ye could*
> *speak with the tongue of angels?*
> —2 NEPHI 32:2

When I ponder this scripture with motherhood in mind, I cannot help but wonder, *How does a mother speak when she speaks with the tongue of angels?* First of all, I like to think that she speaks with obvious love and compassion for her children. That she uses her words to uplift and encourage her children rather than thoughtlessly using her words to put them down. That she seeks to be aware of the power of her words and tone to shape her children's days and even their lives. And that she consciously uses that power to positively affect her children for good.

We have all heard it said that "actions speak louder than words," and yet words can still say so much to our children. Each of us likely remembers something (or perhaps many things) hurtful that one or both of our parents said while we were growing up, something that they may not even remember having said but that has stayed with us nonetheless.

One young man I know can recall being particularly negatively impacted by his father's words and tone many years ago when he was helping him make household repairs. While working together, the son accidentally dropped a tool, and the father thoughtlessly blurted out, "You are so clumsy!" It is doubtful that his father meant "You are so clumsy in every possible way now and forevermore," but given the father's emphatic tone, his obvious frustration, and a lack of further explanation, the son took what his father said to heart and has never quite gotten over seeing himself as a clumsy man, despite his many accomplishments that suggest otherwise.

This is a seemingly simple example, and yet I use it as a reminder to myself to be conscious of what I say to my children and how I say it. I find myself wondering, *If a few words thoughtlessly spoken can have such a negative impact on a child, what difference can a few words, carefully chosen each day, make for our children?* Some days I do better in how I speak to my children than others, but overall I strive to raise my children with words and tones that help rather than hinder them and hopefully heal rather than hurt them. I am thankful to have the gift of the Holy Ghost to guide and support me in my daily interactions with my children.

I have often heard it said that the best gift parents can give their children is to love the other parent. I believe that one of the best ways to show our children that we love their father is to speak kindly to him and about him. Children feel a unique and acute pain when ugly, hurtful words are exchanged between parents or when they are spoken by one parent about the other parent. Parents can hurt each other with their words, but, even more, they can and will hurt their children when they speak cross words about the other parent. This is true whether the parents are in a committed, long-lasting marriage or whether their marriage has ended in divorce. Either way, a mother who speaks with the tongue of angels will seek to be guided by the Holy Ghost in how she speaks to and about the father of her children.

Although soft words and gentle tones generally serve us best when we're talking to our family members, there are times when using strong words and tones may be completely appropriate. When my little ones have put themselves in harm's way—perhaps stepping out into the street or reaching up to touch a hot stove top—I have made it very clear through my tone and words that they need to stop what they are doing—right away.

As my children have moved into their preteen and teen years, there have been times when I have felt the need to speak especially frankly and emphatically with them. I recall a period of time when this was the case with one of my daughters in particular. After what felt like more than sufficient counsel on the part of her father and me to never chat with strangers on the Internet, we found that, despite our careful monitoring and the very public location of our computer, our daughter had been doing just that. I was very concerned and upset that our daughter had disobeyed us in such a way. Through much prayer and many discussions with my husband, we found the strong but loving tone and words we needed to reach past our daughter's naïveté and into her heart to make it clear that she needed to be especially careful when navigating the Internet. I am deeply grateful to have had the Spirit with us to help us know what to say at that time and during other difficult times with our children. Such experiences confirm to me the truth that if we will do our part as parents, it shall be given to us in that same hour what we should say to our children (see Matthew 10:19).

As I think about speaking with the tongue of angels and its implications on motherhood, I cannot help but think about the importance of being true to our word with our kids. I am ashamed to say that I can recall more than a few verbal promises I have made in earnest to my kids but have not kept. I think of myself as being honest in my dealings, and yet I realize that I sometimes tell my kids that I will do certain things, like make cookies or read a story to them, but then I never get to it. This isn't because I don't want to do these things for my kids. Rather, this usually happens when I end up promising to do more than I can possibly deliver in a given day. I am not sure who I let down more when this happens—my kids or myself.

I am happy to report, though, that I am making positive strides in this area. I'm learning to pause before I make a commitment to do something for my kids, to see if what I'm about to commit to doing is realistic given the other demands on my time. I am also learning to communicate to my kids, when appropriate, that I will commit to doing a particular thing for them, but only if it turns out I have the necessary time to do it. Making these changes in how I make and keep my promises has improved my relationship with my kids and taken undue pressure off of me.

When I think of speaking with the tongue of angels, I can't help but think about how most of us moms could be kinder in how we speak about ourselves to ourselves and others. I have felt prompted to make some changes in this area. No one is harder on me than me, and this includes the way I sometimes talk to myself about myself. I think it's okay to reprimand ourselves when we have done wrong and to correct ourselves when we are in need of correction, but maybe sometimes we should do this with more love, more compassion, and more under-standing for ourselves. Perhaps we should speak to ourselves as the Savior would speak to us—with a more pure love.

And, what about the way we speak about ourselves to others? I have come to believe that a little self-deprecating humor can go a very long way in the company of others. It's okay and even good to be humble about ourselves with others, but I have noticed that we moms are sometimes prone to taking humility to extremes when speaking to others about ourselves. We sometimes tend to put ourselves down unnecessarily in conversations, especially with other mothers. What benefit comes from such behavior?

Perhaps we can begin to be kinder to ourselves in how we speak about ourselves by being more gracious in accepting the compliments of others. It seems to me that, more often than not, when someone pays a woman a compliment, especially a mother, she tends to downplay it or even outright reject it. This is something that I used to be especially good at doing. When another mother would compliment me on some aspect of my parenting, I would respond by telling her the many things I didn't think I was doing so well. When a friend would tell me how fit I was looking since I had started jogging, I would say something like, "Oh, but my thighs!" I cannot help but think that angels would speak more kindly about themselves than we moms tend to do.

Two things have finally stopped me from ungraciously diminish-ing or rejecting compliments when they're offered: first, the awkward-ness I have felt when others have rejected a heartfelt compliment I have shared with them and, second, the realization that it serves no one to reject a compliment when one is thoughtfully shared. With these insights in mind, I now strive to simply but graciously accept a compliment when I receive one. In fact, these days, when someone shares a thoughtful remark that especially touches me, I tell them, "I'm going to put your compliment in my treasure box and pull it out on the tough days. Thank you!" This simple change has made such a positive impact on my life and on how I feel about myself as a mother that I now encourage my mothering friends to accept my compliments without qualification when I offer them. I hope this makes a difference for them.

It seems to me that a mother who speaks with the tongue of angels surely speaks well of other mothers. She does not spread gossip nor does she judge other mothers. Rather, she uses her words to uplift other mothers, to encourage them, to comfort and support them in good times and in tough times. When we as mothers seek to speak positively about ourselves and others, we will be giving other mothers permission to be kinder to themselves as well.

We can make a difference for other mothers in how we speak about ourselves and about them, but our greatest opportunity for making an impact with our words is in our own homes by how we speak to our children and our spouses. We can, if we will tap into the power of the Holy Ghost, learn to speak with the tongue of angels. If we come from homes where love was not spoken in words or tones, we can still, with prayer and sincere effort, make progress in creating homes that are built with words of love and kindness. If we will strive to speak with the tongue of angels, we will make of our homes safe havens for our children. And, as we do this, we and our children will experience the peace that comes from having the Spirit dwell strongly in our homes.

Chapter Eighteen

ASKING
FOR WHAT WE NEED

> *Yea, I know that God will give liberally to him that asketh. Yea, my God will give me, if I ask not amiss; therefore I will lift up my voice unto thee; yea, I will cry unto thee, my God, the rock of my righteousness. Behold, my voice shall forever ascend up unto thee, my rock and mine everlasting God. Amen.*
> —2 NEPHI 4:35

I remember vividly the Sunday when my Relief Society president introduced her lesson by saying something to the effect of, "I don't think that we as sisters are very good about asking the Lord for what we need. So, today we're going to talk about asking the Lord for what we need." I was surprised by her approach to the lesson but eager to hear what she had to say. I couldn't help but agree that she had a point. I cannot speak for all the moms I know, but I have to admit that as a mom myself, I could benefit from becoming more conscious of asking the Lord for what I need at this time in my life, namely guidance and help in raising my little ones.

The scriptures are filled with invitations to ask the Lord for what we need—whether that need is for specific answers, insight, guidance, or perhaps a pressing material need or even all of the above. Among the scriptural invitations to ask, my favorites include: "Ask, and it shall be given you" (Matthew 7:7) and "If any of you lack wisdom, let him ask of God, that giveth to all men liberally, and upbraideth not; and it shall be given him" (James 1:5). If you or I ever entertain any doubts about the permissibility and importance of asking the Lord for help and guidance, we need only read the firm reminder, "But ye are commanded in all things to ask of God, who giveth liberally" (D&C 46:7).

Even with these scriptures in mind, we can sometimes neglect to go to the Lord to ask him for what we and our children need. In my case, I think this happens for several reasons. First, because I sometimes get so busy taking care of everyone and everything in my circle of concern that I forget to carve out enough time to really turn to the Lord in a mode of sincere and thoughtful asking. Sometimes I neglect to go to the Lord because I get so caught up in the notion of "it is better to give than to receive" that I feel greedy asking the Lord for anything.

And other times, I think I neglect to go to the Lord because I feel I should be doing better on my own at something before I take it to the Lord. For example, I sometimes struggle with raising my voice unnecessarily with my kids. I am not proud of this but it happens. In my mind, I think I should be able to overcome the yelling on my own and so I have, at times, kept the problem to myself rather than turning to the Lord for help. This seems silly when I take a step back to try to see my situation with more perspective.

It is not the Lord's plan that we become perfect before we come to him. In fact, it is only through him that we can ultimately obtain perfection. Waiting until we are doing better and better and still better again before we go to the Lord seems like the plan of someone who wants us to feel perpetually discouraged and unworthy of the Lord's help, the plan of someone who wants to keep us from getting the very help we are most in need of.

When we neglect to take our concerns and questions as individuals and as parents to the Lord, we are making life harder than it has to be. We are keeping ourselves from the help and inspiration the Lord has promised to give us through the Spirit. On the other hand, when we take our concerns and questions to the Lord and ask sincerely and with the desire to accept the Lord's will for us rather than trying to force our will on him (this is what I think it means to ask "not amiss"), we will be rewarded liberally with answers and with inspiration that will serve us well as we parent our children.

Recently I have taken to heart the admonition to ask the Lord for help, and the resulting experiences have been rewarding. These days, when I jog through my neighborhood in the wee morning hours, I spend time talking to the Lord about each of my five children. I spend some time focusing on each of my kids, starting with the oldest and working my way through to the youngest. As I jog along and pray, I hold a picture in my mind of the child I am praying about. I start by giving thanks for him or her and then pray to the Lord about the worries and questions that come to mind when I think of that child.

When I pray like this for my children, I experience what feels like a floodgate opening in my mind and heart. I find myself awash in love for the child I am praying about and gaining a greater understanding of their needs and of how I, as their mother, can meet those needs. When I finish praying about the questions that come immediately to mind about a particular child, I then pray and ask the Lord, "Is there something more I need to know about this child? Is there something else that you would have me do for this child?" And the Lord, through the Spirit, always gives me some additional inspiration or suggestion for action, whether its to teach one of my children more clearly the importance of choices and consequences or to simply spend more one-on-one time with one or all of my kids.

Lately, I have found these sessions to be especially helpful in parenting one of my daughters who has been struggling with the tempting tug of worldly ways and things. As I've prayed and asked for guidance in mothering her, the Lord has given me many answers such as "remember to focus on the positive while dealing with the challenges" and "be sure to help her prepare to get her patriarchal blessing because she will be deeply affected by the personal and meaningful guidance it will offer her."

I know that one especially helpful bit of inspiration resulted directly from my willingness to ask for guidance regarding this daughter. It was the prompting to find a sister in my ward who would be willing to be an informal mentor and role model to her. When I asked the Lord which sister I should consider, a name came almost immediately to mind—a thirty-year-old sister who is married but not yet a mother herself. This sister has all the energy and pizzazz of my daughter and has put that energy and pizzazz to work in very positive ways—through her talent for artwork, photography, and music as well as through one simple thing that would definitely speak to my daughter at this point in her life: dressing with flair. This sister's attire demonstrates clearly that stylish design, femininity, and modesty can go together beautifully.

When I called this sister to share my thoughts with her and to ask her if she would consider being an active influence in my daughter's life (in whatever ways she felt comfortable), she responded positively. In a short period of time, this sister has made a favorable and lasting impression on my daughter through sharing her love of photography and music and through her overall example, one that leaves me thinking my daughter might choose to be a positive and thoughtful mentor to a young girl herself someday.

I'm getting better at asking the Lord for what I feel my kids and husband need and asking for inspiration in what I can do for them. But, I'm still working on learning to ask him for what I need for myself. I may always struggle with this because it is so hard for me to surrender the notion that I should be charitable to others but completely self-sufficient when it comes to my own needs.

I sometimes imagine what I must look like to my Father in Heaven—perhaps a lot like a willful toddler who thinks she can do everything all by herself. And in some cases, she can. But, in other cases, she would do far better if she would surrender her will to seek the will, guidance, and help of one far wiser and more experienced than herself.

We as moms can try to do it all by ourselves, but there are many times when it is far better to tap into the spiritual power of someone who is far wiser and more experienced than we are. Let us go to the Lord and ask in behalf of the needs of our children and our spouses, but let us also go to the Lord to ask for what we need as well, whether that need is for a calmer voice as we work with our children or to find a way to get some much-needed rest. In my experience, the Lord may not always give us what we want in the exact time frame we want it in, but he will always give us what we need.

Praying and asking in behalf of our children and our spouses is a wonderful gift of love we give to them. But I am beginning to see that praying and asking for what we need for ourselves is no less a gift of love to those around us. In fact, I think it's something that we should become good at doing. After all, when we seek the Lord's help in having our needs met, we will be better able to play a meaningful part in meeting the needs of those we love most.

Chapter Nineteen

TURNING OUR WEAKNESSES
INTO STRENGTHS

> *And if men come unto me I will show unto them*
> *their weakness. I give unto men weakness that they*
> *may be humble; and my grace is sufficient for all men*
> *that humble themselves before me; for if they humble*
> *themselves before me, and have faith in me, then will*
> *I make weak things become strong unto them.*
> —ETHER 12:27

I don't know about you, but I can just imagine the Lord having said something like this to me years ago: "Become a mom and I will show unto you your weaknesses." This is not to say that I was perfect before I became a mother—perhaps in my imagination, but never in reality. Even so, being a mother has definitely brought my weaknesses to the surface and magnified them. The bright side to becoming so clear on my weaknesses is that such clarity has served as one of my most compelling and humbling invitations to spiritual growth.

As discouraged as we can become when faced head-on with our weaknesses as parents, there is great hope to be found in the Lord's promise that if we will humble ourselves before him and have faith in him, he will then make our weaknesses become our strengths. I have tapped into the power of this promise many times during my years as a mother. And each time the Lord has supported, guided, and strengthened me in making the changes I've needed to make. Sometimes, I am able to make a needed change almost immediately; other times turning a weakness into a strength takes months and even years. However long it takes to make necessary changes, I can tell you that the Lord will be there for us, cheering us on and giving us strength. He is a God of hope; he will not forsake us.

During my early years as a mom, I became acquainted for the first time with the realities of not getting enough sleep—ever. I remember well reading one researcher's assertion that a new mom may lose up to seven hundred hours of sleep before her baby's first birthday. Anyone who has parented children past the age of one knows that sleep loss doesn't stop there. Being chronically low on sleep magnifies my weaknesses, making me forgetful, short-tempered with my kids, impatient with myself, and a poor conversationalist as I attempt to speak clear, complete thoughts with anyone, including my kids. The bottom line is that being a tired mom generally makes me a grumpy mom, and that's not the kind of mom my kids want or need.

On the days when I am feeling especially exhausted, I turn to the Lord for help in being the calm, strong, and clear-thinking mom my kids need that day rather than succumbing to the grumpy mom that rises so easily to the surface when I am tired. My years of experience as a mom have certainly made me better at riding out the inevitable waves of fatigue, but my experience alone isn't enough to help me navigate those sleep-deprived days as well as I want to or need to.

Whenever I turn to the Lord in faith to ask for help in overcoming my grumpiness and fatigue for the sake of my kids, he is there for me. Through the Spirit, I have received comfort and energy on those fatigue-filled days as well as clarity of thought and feelings of calm that I could not have mustered so easily on my own. I think that what has helped me the most on such days is the prompting of the Spirit to find the best way through the next hour rather than allowing myself to become overwhelmed with the thought of getting through the rest of the day. I confess that I am always especially thankful on the days when the Lord blesses me with the miracle of squeezing in a much-needed nap.

For a person like me who is very results-oriented, parenthood is an ongoing invitation to stretch spiritually and emotionally. After all, so much of parenthood is really about being engaged in the process of raising our children rather than being in the mode of measuring visible results. Thinking about the results we want for our children, whether those results are a clean bedroom or, far more important, a strong testimony, has its place, but I've learned that focusing too much on the ends we have in mind can, if we're not careful, rob our children and us of the joy available to us in the here and now.

As I have sought guidance from the Lord in overcoming my tendency to focus too much on getting to the results with my kids, he has blessed me with greater perspective, understanding, and patience. Slowly, through prayer, exercising faith in the Lord, and much effort on my part to change, I am becoming a parent who is more fully engaged in doing what I need to do with my kids right now, while learning to trust that good results will likely follow focused, unrushed efforts.

Few of us are inclined to run and ask friends and family members to point out our weaknesses as parents, but we should not hesitate to go to the Lord. After all, he promises to not only show us our weaknesses, but, if we are humble and teachable, he promises to make our weak things become strong. I find it especially reassuring to know that this promise is given in the context of the Lord's perfect love for us.

I have to admit that I haven't always taken full advantage of the Lord's promise to turn our weaknesses into our strengths. Sometimes, when I become aware of a weakness I have as a parent, I hesitate to seek help from the Lord. Deep down, I feel I should be able to overcome the weakness on my own. This was certainly the case when my oldest child moved into her teen years and my patience began to run particularly thin. With all of my years of parenting experience, I was quite sure I could figure out the teen scene on my own. I couldn't have been more wrong. As it turns out, the skills I had gained while parenting my young children hardly prepared me for parenting a teenager. After experiencing a rather rocky start as the mother to a teen due, in great part, to my lack of patience, I knew that I needed the Lord's help more than ever in raising my teenagers.

As I have sought the Lord's help and exercised faith in him, he has blessed me with an awareness of what I am doing that's not working and what I can do differently as a mother of teens. In particular, he has blessed me with the understanding that, as much as I want results now with my teenagers, mothering teens is, in part, an exercise in planting seeds now that may not bear fruit for years to come.

Overall, as I have learned to trust in the Lord to guide me through the teenage years, I have received insights that I would not have otherwise received, felt inspired to take action that I would not have otherwise taken, and enjoyed a closer relationship with my daughter than I otherwise would have. One of the best and most effective inspirations I have received is to take advantage of those late nights when I am tired but when my daughter, after her friends are gone and the house has settled, wants to talk. Those late night sessions have done much to strengthen our relationship. By having faith in the Lord and following his counsel, I am hopefully laying a strong and vibrant foundation for seeing all of my kids through their teenage years.

Even now, when I think of facing my weaknesses as a parent, I feel a little overwhelmed. I remind myself though that it is Satan's plan for us to become overwhelmed when confronting our weaknesses. And, in contrast, it is the Lord's plan to give us encouragement and strength as we prayerfully seek in faith to make the changes we need to make as parents.

Over the years, as I have sought the Lord's guidance in overcoming my weaknesses, he has blessed me with the reminder that we as moms need to be sure to recognize what we are already doing well. When we recognize and honor our strengths, we will find it easier to confront and overcome our weaknesses, to transform them into our strengths. As we follow the Lord's plan for becoming the best moms we can become by overcoming our weaknesses, even making them our strengths, we will be setting an important example for our children to follow. For we will be showing them, through our actions, how they too can seek the Lord's help in turning their very weaknesses into their greatest strengths.

Chapter Twenty

TRUSTING IN THE LORD MORE THAN IN THE EXPERTS

> *O Lord, I have trusted in thee and I will trust in thee forever. I will not put my trust in the arm of flesh; for I know that cursed is he that putteth his trust in the arm of flesh. Yea, cursed is he that putteth his trust in man or maketh flesh his arm.*
> —2 NEPHI 4:34

Sometimes I find myself wondering just how many experts it takes to raise one child. It seems to me that if we let popular parenting magazines, TV shows, and radio talk shows answer this question for us, we will find that we can never have enough. I believe that experts can provide us with crucial support as we raise our children, particularly if we are raising a child who has special needs. But, generally speaking, I think that we as parents sometimes give too much weight to the opinions of the experts, allowing them to become "the authority," the final word in our efforts to raise our children well.

When I find myself tuning into the experts more than I tune into myself, I remind myself that as knowledgeable and well-intended as they may be, the experts cannot possibly care about my children as much as I do, whether they know them or not. And, truth be told, as well as I know my kids and as much as I love them, there is someone who knows and loves them even more than I do: the Lord. My husband and I together make a solid and caring parenting team. Even so, our team is incomplete without regular guidance from the Lord.

In my early days as a mother, I did not understand the importance of seeking guidance from the Lord as fully as I do now. I was a less active member of the Church who had recently gone through a divorce and found myself feeling particularly vulnerable to the child-rearing philosophies that were in current fashion and much touted by popular experts. I wanted to do a good job raising my young daughter but felt very much alone in doing so. I put a lot of pressure on myself, feeling that I had to make up for the fact that my daughter's father was absent from her life. I wanted my daughter to know how much she was loved and how completely worthy she was of being loved despite her father's absence. With these goals in mind, I developed a parenting style that was, in retrospect, overly child-centered. I had become so concerned with my daughter's self-esteem, so attentive not just to her needs but to her wants, that it seems I did a disservice to us both.

As I became active in the Church again, I was reminded of what help and guidance is available to us as parents through the Spirit if we will seek it. As I studied the scriptures, listened to the inspired words of Church leaders, and prayed more thoughtful, heartfelt prayers, I gained the knowledge and power I needed to make some needed changes in how I was raising my daughter. With the help of the Spirit, I developed a parenting style that was firmer but still loving. I continued to be attentive to my daughter's needs but helped her to put her wants into perspective—teaching her that sometimes you get to have what you want and other times you don't and that sometimes not getting what you want may be the very best thing for you.

By consciously seeking the Lord's expertise and wisdom through prayer, scripture study, and listening to the inspired words of Church leaders, I found many ways to teach my daughter the beauty of living the gospel in our daily lives. Together, we learned much about serving others by taking meals to families in need in our ward and through our weekly visits to a nearby nursing home where we made some wonderful elderly friends.

As prompted by the Spirit, I worked to teach my daughter other gospel lessons as well, including the importance of doing unto others as she would want them to do unto her and the importance of accepting the Lord's invitation to make a difference in the lives of others by letting her light shine through her testimony and talents. As I learned to trust in the Lord more than in the experts, my confidence as a parent soared and my daughter grew in maturity and spirit.

Over the years, I have learned that when a child is in crisis, getting help from the right expert can make all the difference. Even so, several years ago, some friends reminded me of how important it is to pause even in the midst of a crisis to seek the Lord's guidance in getting help for our children. This couple's teenage daughter had become addicted to drugs and had lost control of every aspect of her life. The parents, realizing that their daughter's problem had grown beyond their ability to solve it alone, sought guidance from a highly respected medical professional. The professional recommended a renowned drug treatment center where she felt they could get the help they needed for their daughter.

Relying on this expert's recommendation and without much additional thought or prayer, these parents, feeling desperate, had their daughter admitted almost immediately to the suggested treatment center. In the course of their daughter's treatment they realized that this particular treatment center had not been a good choice for their child after all. Unfortunately for them, the treatment program was geared more toward the needs of adults who had been addicted to drugs and alcohol for many years than to the needs of an impressionable adolescent. And, to make matters worse, the parents discovered that the values espoused by the professionals who ran the program conflicted significantly with their own values. When these parents had their daughter discharged from the program, they felt that she was in greater need of help, not less. At that low point in their parenting life, they made a commitment, more than ever before, to invite the Lord to guide them as they made the decisions that would impact any of their children's future well-being.

In my experience as a mother, the "child-rearing experts" in our lives do not always come with academic or professional credentials in tow. Instead, they sometimes come in the form of well-meaning family members and friends who feel sure they know what is best for our children and don't hesitate to advise us. What they have to say about one or more of our children may be the very thing we need to hear, the direct answer to an earnest prayer. But then again, it may not be. No matter how compelling the thoughts are that they share, no matter how sure they may seem about their opinions, we owe it to our children and ourselves to check in with the Lord to confirm the truth and relevance of what they share. He will not allow us to be led astray in raising our children if we seek his guidance and heed it.

There will surely be times in our parenting lives when we will want to actively seek outside expertise in meeting the needs of our children. I know that my children have benefited when my husband and I have sought the help of the right expert at the right time, whether for help in dealing with a child's learning disability or for a particular medical concern. We are most likely to succeed in seeking outside help for our children when we follow the Lord's admonition to do our homework, to study the situation out in our minds, and to then take our solutions, including any choices we make about seeking outside help, to the Lord for confirmation (see D&C 9:8).

We can find comfort in knowing that the Lord has promised to answer our inquiries. He has said, "If it is right I shall cause that your bosom shall burn within you; therefore, you shall feel that it is right. But if it be not right you shall have no such feelings, but you shall have a stupor of thought that shall cause you to forget the thing which is wrong" (D&C 9:8–9). It is my experience that the Lord indeed provides us with a burning in our bosoms when we arrive at the right answer for one of our children. I have experienced this burning in my bosom most often as a feeling of clear confidence and comfort with the answers my husband and I arrive at for one of my children after much studying, pondering, and prayer. As we seek direction from the Lord and follow his counsel, we will find it easier to navigate our way through the myriad experts and child-rearing philosophies so prevalent in our day and time. Even better, when we put our trust in the Lord to guide and support us in raising our children, we will be taking the best opportunity available to us to become the most helpful and caring earthly experts our children could ever have.

Chapter Twenty-One

LISTENING TO OUR CHILDREN AS THEY LISTEN TO THE SPIRIT

> *Little children do have words given unto them many times, which confound the wise and the learned.*
>
> —ALMA 32:23

In the years before I became a mother, I had a head full of theories and preconceived notions about what parenthood would be like. I was right in several respects, such as the fact that I would love my children dearly every day and like them quite well on most days and the reality that my life would change forever on the day my first child was born whether I felt completely ready for that change or not. On the other hand, I was wrong on more than a few things about parenthood, most notably that getting enough sleep while raising kids would be no big deal and that I would be *the teacher* to my children and that they would, of course, be *my students.*

It took about two nights after the birth of my oldest daughter to figure out that I was completely wrong on the sleep issue and not much more time to realize that my children would be, in some respects, my teachers as much as I was theirs. Even as babies, my kids taught me lessons in patience, lessons about putting others' needs before my own, and the truth about how meaningful it can be to serve one of Heavenly Father's little ones, even in the smallest respects.

These early lessons were invaluable as they served to smooth away the rough edges of my self-centeredness. I sometimes wonder what I would be like now if I hadn't had children to soften my spirit over the years. My kids' roles as teachers in our home have expanded even more as they've each learned to talk. Each one of them, down to my toddler, has taken me off guard with their observations, their inspirations, and their surprising grasp of spiritual truths. I have long been familiar with the scriptural passage that proclaims that "little children do have words given unto them many times, which confound the wise and the learned" (Alma 32:23). However, experiencing this spiritual truth firsthand in my own home has given me an enormous appreciation for the difference even our young children can make in our understanding of life on earth and our purpose here.

I can still vividly recall the words of my oldest daughter, who was three at the time, when I told her that I was pregnant and that she would become a big sister in just a few more months. Her eyes lit up immediately, and she broke into an enormous smile as she reached over to pat my stomach and exclaim, "Mommy, I love that baby in your tummy! Who is it?" I couldn't help but laugh at her sincere exclamation and question. I told her that I too loved the baby in my tummy and that, like her, I didn't know who the baby was going to be but that we would find out together.

Almost twelve years later, now the mother of five, I still marvel at the simple but powerful thoughts my daughter expressed that day. We as parents often love our children before they come to earth even though we don't likely know who they are yet. And we're certainly filled with wonder at the thought of who they might be as we anticipate their arrival. What an incredible experience it is to get to know them once they're here as we watch their spirits unfold and blossom over the years. They may have their dad's eyes or their aunt's artistic bent, but, in truth, they are each one of a kind; there is no one else on earth exactly like them. I stand in awe of this fact about my children every day.

At the time I became a parent, I felt somewhat wise and fairly learned. But, looking back now, I realize that I was really just a beginner at life with much ahead to learn. Nevertheless, my children have taught me that even the youngest of beginners can have inspiration and wisdom given to them if they are open to the whisperings of the Spirit. Each of my children has listened to those whisperings at important times and shared what they've heard in ways that have made a profound and lasting impact on me.

I remember one such occasion when, without thinking, I blurted out something rude and insensitive to my third daughter, who was seven at the time. She is generally thick-skinned, but my comments had bruised a tender spot, and I knew immediately that I had blown it. Before I could apologize, my daughter ran up the stairs to her room with a swell of tears held barely in check. As I started up the stairs, I prayed to Heavenly Father that he would help me to know how best to apologize to my daughter and how to undo the hurt I had so thoughtlessly inflicted.

As I turned into her bedroom, I found my daughter huddled in the blankets on her bed, tears streaming down her face. I sat down beside her, pulled her into my arms, and told her how sorry I was for what I had said. She smiled through her tears and said, "Mommy, it's okay. If you can't make mistakes, you can't make anything."

I was supposed to be comforting my daughter, but, as it turned out, she had already received comfort from the Spirit and was passing that comfort on to me. She was absolutely right in what she shared with me. If we do not allow ourselves to make mistakes, we cannot do or make much of anything. If we as moms become so wrapped up in being perfect every step of the way, we will likely hold ourselves back, so much so, that we will create a bland and possibly even joyless existence with our families.

Another time, more recently, I had an experience with my four-year-old son that reached deep into my heart. It happened one Wednesday morning when we were the only two at home. I was straightening the house while he played with his building blocks. While tidying the family room, I felt a tug on my pant leg and looked down to see my little boy looking up rather earnestly into my face. When he had my full attention, he said, "Mom, I have something to tell you. In Primary on Sunday, Sister Harrison taught me about Joseph Smith and how he went to the Sacred Grove to pray. At first things got very dark, and then they got very bright because Heavenly Father and Jesus Christ came to visit him . . . (long pause here) . . . Mom, sometimes we need to pray with others, but sometimes we need to go off and pray by ourselves." He said nothing more but smiled, hugged me, and went off to play again, leaving me to ponder what he had shared. Our house may have been relatively low on people that morning, but it was absolutely full of the Spirit.

Each of my five children has had words given unto them by the Spirit at times that have absolutely confounded me, touched my heart, and transformed my understanding and appreciation of our time on earth. In talking with other mothers, it is clear to me that my kids are not the exception. Every mother I know has stories to tell of the inspired words her children have shared and the difference those words have made in their family life.

If we will listen closely to our young children, acknowledge and value the inspiration they share with us, and help them to understand the source of that inspiration, we will be helping them to lay the foundation for a life that is more likely to be lived in tune with the Spirit. And what a wonderful gift this can be to give our children—a gift that requires no grand gestures or fanfare but rather begins with the simple act of listening to our little ones and acknowledging the inspired wisdom they will surely share.

Chapter Twenty-Two

DOING ALL THINGS
IN WISDOM AND ORDER

> *And see that all these things are done in wisdom and order; for it is not requisite that a man should run faster than he has strength. And again, it is expedient that he should be diligent, that thereby he might win the prize; therefore, all things must be done in order.*
> —MOSIAH 4:27

When I think of the Savior's time on earth, I envision him as being calm and unrushed, a healing presence as he diligently goes about doing his Father's work. In contrast, when I envision myself and so many other mothers I know going through our days I see, in my mind's eye, a mom who's rushing to get it all done as she sprints headlong through her waking hours. Despite her best efforts, she never seems to arrive at the finish line where she can say, "I got it all done," but she never stops trying. She wants to be a calm and loving presence in her home but sometimes ends up fostering an atmosphere of anxiety more than one of peace with all her rushing.

So, how do we as moms do it all, and do it in a reasonably calm state, when there is always so much to be done? Several years ago,

I found myself especially laboring over this question as I struggled through some particularly hectic and stressful days. We had just moved to a new city where I was without my familiar support network and where I did not yet feel comfortable asking others for help. My husband, who has always been a big help on the home front, was suddenly away much of the time with unexpected, job-related travels and some heavy Church responsibilities. I was committed to getting my act together on my own but was having a difficult time juggling all the balls that my act seemed to require.

Every day I would get up and try harder to make some headway on my lengthy and ever-growing to-do list. I worked almost nonstop to get our new home in order; to get our kids settled into a new community with new doctors, teachers, friends, and so forth; and to manage the day to day needs of our household only to feel at the end of each day that I had not accomplished nearly as much as I should have that day.

I have heard it said that within every trial we face, there exists an invitation to be blessed. And during this challenging time, the Lord blessed me with the clear impression that if I wanted to create greater order in my life overall, I needed to create greater spiritual order first. I had been saying my prayers regularly and studying my scriptures faithfully, and yet there was room for improvement, room to go deeper in my prayers to the Lord and room to become more focused, more thorough in my scripture study.

As I made seeking spiritual order a greater priority in my daily life through more intensive scripture study and more meditative prayers, I felt an easing of my load and an ordering of my days. I felt the truth of the Savior's promise, "Come unto me, all ye that labour and are heavy laden, and I will give you rest" (Matthew 11:28). I began to see that this particularly chaotic time in a new city would indeed pass. I also began to recognize that some of the things on my to-do list that had seemed enormously important weren't really so important after all. What was important was the prayerful prioritizing of my children's needs for physical, emotional, and spiritual nurturance. I could, I realized, meet their needs without having to accomplish every last item on my to-do list. What a relief it was to realize this through the inspiration of the Spirit.

In my experience as a mother, the pressure I feel to move faster than I have strength is not always based on external circumstances such as a cross-country move. There have been times in my life when outside pressure to get things done has been at a minimum; but I have pressured myself nonetheless to do more than is reasonably possible in a given period of time. At such times, I think I have taken too much to heart the scriptural admonition to be anxiously engaged in a good cause (see D&C 58:27). I have sometimes interpreted this scripture to mean that we should see just how many good causes we can become anxiously engaged in—all at the same time and all without any consideration for what we can reasonably do while caring for our kids. Without exception, there has been a high price to pay when I have forgotten the counsel to do all things in wisdom and order. Through painful experience, I have learned that becoming a severely burned-out mom does little good for anyone.

So what is it that drives us as moms to run faster than we have strength, to attempt to accomplish more than we can reasonably accomplish while still allowing ourselves sufficient time for rest? In part, I think the answer is that we have big hearts. With such big hearts, we cannot help but see the needs and, yes, the wants of those around us. And oh how we want to meet those needs and even most of those wants. As long as we keep in mind the counsel to do things in wisdom and order, our big hearts will be to our advantage and the advantage of those around us. But, if we ignore or lose sight of the counsel to use wisdom and order in our doing, we will inevitably experience the downsides of such big hearts (perhaps in the form of exhaustion and burn-out) as will those we love and want to care for.

While big hearts can sometimes be our downfall if we're not careful, there's something else that sometimes drives us to run faster than we have strength, to do more than we realistically can, that thing is fear—the fear that we are not doing our part as well as Sister So-and-So over in the next pew, the fear that we will not meet with the approval of others if we do not do more and more and yet more again, the fear that we will never be good enough as a wife, a mother, a Church member, a sister, a friend, or even as a daughter of God if we cease striving long enough to catch our breaths, to renew our spirits and bodies.

A little fear can be a good thing by motivating us to do our part. But, when we allow ourselves to become consumed with fear and driven by fear, we may unintentionally hurt rather than help ourselves and those around us with our anxious striving. I find it comforting to recall the spiritual truth found in 2 Timothy 1:7, "For God hath not given us the spirit of fear, but of power, and of love, and of a sound mind." When we do what is before us with wisdom and in order, we are better able to tap into the spirit of power and love and to retain sound minds as we do our part.

So, in a world that seems bent on pressuring us to see how fast we can run through our days, how do we set our own pace? How do we stay focused on what's most important rather than allowing ourselves to become frantically busy with what's less important or perhaps not really important after all? Alma's counsel to Helaman provides what I have come to think of as the definitive answer to this question, "Counsel with the Lord in all thy doings, and he will direct thee for good" (see Alma 37:37). In heeding this counsel, I am learning to better let go of my earthly notions of what I should be accomplishing each day in favor of focusing on what the Lord would most have me do.

To this end, I strive to set aside time at the beginning of each day to make a list of what I hope to get done that day. After I make my list I take the time to nourish myself with the scriptures and to consult with the Lord in prayer about my goals for the day. When I return to my list, I return with perspective. I feel more focused, more at peace in establishing my priorities for the day—priorities that are set by the Lord and priorities that, with his direction, I can work toward with greater calm and energy.

I believe it is no small thing that King Benjamin counseled his people, and hence us, twice in the same verse to do things in wisdom and order. Doing things with wisdom and order is a skill that takes prayer, time, resolve, and, it seems, reminders to develop. When I find myself tempted to do too much, to run faster than I have strength, I pause long enough to take a breath and to check in with the Lord. Through the Spirit, the Lord can give us the strength we need to run as fast as is called for, but thankfully he can also help us to recognize the times when less speed is called for rather than more.

Chapter Twenty-Three

REMEMBERING OUR BLESSINGS

And now, I ask, what great blessings has he bestowed upon us? Can ye tell?

—ALMA 26:2

Mothering may be the most challenging work we ever do. When things are going well, it can be easy to parent with our whole hearts. When we're facing particularly tough days or weeks and find ourselves feeling blue, it may not be so easy. Regardless of our circumstances, we are more likely to raise our children with compassionate, appreciative, and open hearts when we consciously weave gratitude into our days.

For some, a truly thankful heart comes naturally. For others, like me, gratitude is something best worked at deliberately. Otherwise we tend to focus on what's not working, on what problems we have yet to solve, or on how we wish things could be somehow different.

Many years ago, while I was going through a difficult divorce and facing an uncertain future as a single mother to my young daughter, I learned the power of gratitude to color my days. Despite the challenges I faced at the time, I made the decision to actively focus my attention more on what was going well in my life rather than becoming overwhelmed by everything that wasn't. In the hopes that it would help, I started a gratitude journal where I began to make notes of the large and the small blessings I was thankful for. I made no huge, super-focused effort to count my blessings; rather, I simply wrote them down whenever they came to mind. I also made more focused time in my prayers to express thanks to Heavenly Father for my blessings. I was surprised by the difference such a small shift in focus made in the tone of my days. My growing awareness of my blessings and increased acknowledgment of them diluted my difficulties and positively shaped my daily experience, including my parenting daily experience.

Becoming more conscious of my blessings changed my life because it changed my view of my life. By exercising gratitude, I experienced a greater sense of abundance—one that made the downsides of life seem smaller, less daunting, and more manageable. Whatever circumstances we're facing we can usually find that there's still much to be thankful for. I believe that we create our mothering lives by what we choose to focus on. If we dwell mostly on the challenges as we raise our children, we'll likely define our parenting lives as hard, burdensome, and even unhappy. But if we will take actions like keeping a gratitude journal of what we're thankful for each day as parents and making our prayers, in great part, prayers of thanksgiving for the little things while raising our children, we will become more mindful of the genuine happiness available to us every day.

Children benefit from knowing that their mother is raising them with a grateful heart. Even better, children learn how to create joyful lives for themselves when invited to awaken their own hearts by consciously practicing gratitude.

Some years ago, after I remarried, my husband and I, hoping to nurture gratitude in our children, started a year-round "Family Thanksgiving Journal." We do not write in it as frequently as I write in my personal gratitude journal, but we make entries often enough that it makes a noticeable difference in our family life. We keep our gratitude journal near the dinner table and when someone remembers, we pull it out and invite everyone to share what they're thankful for while one person records the shared thoughts in our journal. This tradition has helped our children to become aware of their many blessings rather than leaving them to dwell on all the "things" advertisers tell them they absolutely must have. My husband and I have found this tradition to be especially insightful because it has helped us to better understand what touches the heart of each member of our family, whether it's an afternoon spent picking wildflowers or the kind act of a sibling. An added benefit is that our family gratitude journal serves as a priceless family history.

While I have worked diligently over the years to teach my children the importance of expressing gratitude for the blessings their Father in Heaven has given them, the lessons have not always gone one way. My children have taught me much about counting my blessings as well. I remember one Thanksgiving season several years ago when I was feeling especially discouraged. Our family had been through a particularly tough year financially with the loss of my husband's job, a sobering job search, an unwanted move, the depletion of our hard-earned savings, and a terribly uncertain financial future.

I wanted to put on a good face for the sake of my kids but was having a hard time doing so when our immediate financial future looked so bleak. Despite my usually grateful heart, I was struggling to see the bright side in our situation. I knew that I needed to gain some perspective and, thankfully, one of my children reminded me, through her example, of the benefits that come from counting my blessings regardless of my circumstances.

Late one evening shortly before Thanksgiving, while I was tidying the house, my husband returned home after picking up our then eight-year-old daughter from a church activity. My daughter has always enjoyed the Achievement Day activities at church, but this time she looked positively radiant as she swept into the house calling out for me. "Mom, Mom, I want to show you what we did at church tonight! You have to see." She indicated that this was not something she could share with me while I was standing up, so she asked me to sit down with her at the kitchen table. When I sat down, she pulled out a long sheet of paper and laid it in front of me, exclaiming, "Look, Mom, I have 129 things to be thankful for!"

"Wow," I expressed in wonder as I looked closely at her list. Yes, indeed, she had found 129 things to be thankful for—everything from each of her family members to the lush but sparse trees dotting our neighborhood. My daughter explained that she had taken part in a contest at church to see which girl could think of the most things to be thankful for, and she was excited to announce that she had won. "It was easy mom! I have so much to be thankful for!" I was surprised by my daughter's lengthy list since she was well aware of our financial struggles. She had borne the impact of them firsthand, yet she hadn't let the tough times keep her from remembering her blessings. I was touched by her example and felt that I would do well to follow it.

When I sat down some days later to create my own list of 129 things to be thankful for, I made some unexpected and important discoveries. Not surprisingly, I included my husband and kids on my list as well as things like our home and our mostly reliable cars, but there was another area of blessings that surfaced as well. I found myself grateful for the many experiences that I had enjoyed with my family over the last year—experiences that had cost little or nothing at all.

That tough year had certainly stripped me of the sense of financial security that I held so dear, but it had not taken all the good times with it. In fact, the tough times had caused me to become more conscious of creating the good times we had enjoyed together as a family—everything from a trip to the lake to play on the rocks along the shore to the story nights lit only by candlelight. I was so struck by the good memories that came up that I couldn't help but wonder if, in a way, the tough times hadn't really been a gift after all. My daughter had taught me a beautiful lesson about having gratitude even during difficult times.

I am so grateful for the scriptural reminder to "live in thanksgiving daily" (Alma 34:38). In these latter days, it could be so easy to live our entire lives with the feeling that we never have enough, that we need more and more and yet more again to finally be happy as individuals and as families. It is not just our children who are susceptible to the advertising, media, and peer pressure that is so prevalent in our society today. We as parents would do well to examine such pressure with a critical eye and to see it for what it is and then do our part to nurture a sense of gratitude in our hearts and in our children's hearts. If we will seek to live in thanksgiving with our children today and every day, we will be giving them a truly meaningful gift—the gift of knowing that they are abundantly blessed by a Father in Heaven who loves them.

Chapter Twenty-Four

MOTHERING
WITH SPIRITUAL POWER

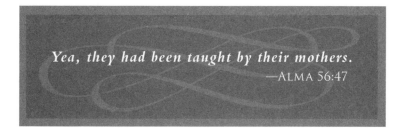

Yea, they had been taught by their mothers.
—ALMA 56:47

M y sister Becky recently gave me a gift that took my breath away the moment I laid eyes on it. It was, in my estimation, a wonder to behold. She had presented me with a visual representation of four generations of my matriarchal line. The lovely dark cherry frame that displayed her gift was separated into four panels, each containing a black and white portrait of one of the women in my matriarchal line. The photographs are close-up, capturing beautifully the face of each woman and just enough of her clothes to see the period of history she was from.

In the far right panel is a photo of me in my late twenties, my face aglow with four months of pregnancy (with my second daughter). To the left of my picture is a picture of my mother, Joyce, looking like a

Hollywood starlet in her high school graduation portrait. Her chest-nut-brown hair is styled into a perfectly coiffed bouffant, and she is wrapped in a faux mink stole, looking radiant with youth. To the left of my mother's picture is a picture of her mother, Laurleen, likely in her mid-twenties. Laurleen looks like Shirley Temple all grown up: creamy skin; short, wavy brown hair; an earnest smile; and innocent eyes that are wise beyond her years. And to the left of Laurleen's pic-ture is a picture of Hannah Sophia, Laurleen's mother and my great-grandmother, a beautiful young pioneer immigrant from Denmark. Hannah Sophia looks like a romantic in her portrait, perhaps a poet, dressed in a high-collared blouse trimmed with white lace, her dark curly hair swept back into a bun.

When I look at this collection of photographs so thoughtfully arranged by my sister, I feel a deep sense of connection with the three women whose pictures are displayed alongside mine. I know this sense of connection is, in part, due to our shared genes. After all, when I look at the picture of my grandmother I see the tilt of my chin. When I look at the picture of my great-grandmother, I see a reflective nature in her eyes, a nature I suspect I inherited from her. And when I look at the picture of my own mother, I see a smile that reminds me of the joy for life my mother and I share.

It is clear to me that I have inherited much from these women in the way of my physical attributes and personality. Even so, I recognize that there is something else that I have inherited from them as well, something far more valuable to me than DNA and something that fills my heart with immense gratitude and joy. And that something is a deep and abiding testimony of and love for the gospel of Jesus Christ.

It was my great-great grandmother Cecilia (Hannah Sophia's mother) who first introduced the gospel into my matriarchal line. She, along with her husband, listened to the missionaries in their humble farmhouse in Denmark and, feeling the truth of what they shared, chose to be baptized into the Church.

In reading Cecilia's personal history, it is clear to me that she made every effort to teach and raise her children in the gospel. And then her daughter, Hannah Sophia, in turn, made every effort to teach and raise her own children in the gospel. Sadly though, Hannah Sophia's daughter, Laurleen, did not have the opportunity to raise her four chil-dren—my mother and her three siblings—to adulthood. She died in childbirth when my mother was just three-years-old. Nevertheless, it is well known in our family that Laurleen had a strong and rich testimony of the gospel. In reading her personal history and in listening to the stories of those who knew her, it is clear to me that she was a devoted follower and servant of the Lord during her years on earth, whether in her service as a full-time missionary in her early twenties or as the mother to her four young children.

Although my mother did not have the blessing of being raised to adulthood by her mother, she tells me that she has always felt deeply the legacy of her mother's testimony and faith, and that her mother's testimony and faith have done much to sustain her during the difficult times she has faced in her own life.

My mother has, more than once, expressed gratitude for Thelma, the stepmother who raised her and her siblings, for making sure that she and her siblings attended church regularly and that family prayer and scripture study were fixtures in their home and family life.

I feel immensely blessed to have been raised by a mother who was committed to nourishing her children in the gospel of Jesus Christ. My mother will be the first to say that she wasn't perfect as a mother, but after years of being a mother myself, I think, "Who is?" How grateful I am that my mother sought to actively and consistently teach my three sisters and me the gospel by taking us to church regularly, holding family home evenings, sharing her testimony often, filling our house with uplifting music, taking advantage of "teaching moments," and so on. I was indeed taught by my mother.

And coming from a mother, indeed a long line of mothers who have sought to raise their children in the gospel, I want nothing less for my own children. Even as I write this, I realize that I have some terrific mothering friends in the Church who did not have the blessing of being actively raised in the gospel of Jesus Christ. But having found and embraced the gospel of Jesus Christ somewhere along the way, they too want nothing less for their children than to give them the very best in the way of the spiritual nourishment and education the gospel has to offer.

My friends Helen, Becky, Sandi, and Victoria are all converts to the gospel. Their conversion stories vary in the details but are equally compelling in their power. While in their youth or during their early adult years, each of these women searched intently for greater spiritual truth and light. When each of them came into contact with the gospel and studied and prayed about it in earnest, she knew she had found what she had been looking for. And, as mothers to their own children, these women have experienced great joy in sharing the gospel with their children while they are yet in their youth.

As mothers, most of us would love to be able to prepare our children in detail for every challenge they may encounter during their earthly lives. But this is not only unrealistic, it is impossible, especially considering our increasingly complex world with its rapidly developing technologies and ever-growing wickedness.

I have found that the story of the stripling warriors in the Book of Mormon provides wonderful inspiration for how to prepare our children for futures that we cannot fully predict. The mothers of the stripling warriors likely did not know their sons would go off to war someday, and yet their sons were well prepared for the battle they had to fight against the Lamanites. In Helaman's epistle to Moroni, Helaman reports that the stripling warriors had never fought, "and yet they did not fear death. And they did think more upon the liberty of their fathers than they did upon their lives; yea, they had been taught by their mothers, that if they would not doubt, God would deliver them" (Alma 56:47). Helaman reports further that "they [the stripling warriors] rehearsed unto me the words of their mothers, saying: We do not doubt our mothers knew it" (Alma 56:48).

It is unlikely that the mothers of the stripling warriors educated their sons specifically in the art of war. But, it is clear from the words of their sons that they gave them a solid education in matters of the Spirit—an education that would see them through war or whatever other challenges they would face in life. Like the mothers of the stripling warriors, we cannot prepare our children in detail for every situation they will encounter in their lives. But, like the mothers of the stripling warriors, we can prepare our children spiritually so they can make their way through whatever challenges they may face during their lives on earth.

The Lord's Church provides us with an abundance of divine guidance and many important tools to help us raise our children in truth and light and so to prepare them for their futures. I find the proclamation on the family to be an especially powerful reminder of what I need to focus on in raising my children. The proclamation states that "successful marriages and families [and lives] are established and maintained on principles of faith, prayer, repentance, forgiveness, respect, love, compassion, work, and wholesome recreational activities." When I feel overwhelmed in what I should focus on in teaching my children, I return to this wise counsel and seek to heed it.

Raising our children will be the most important work we will ever do here on earth. It is a sacred work. And it is a challenging work. As wonderful as raising children can be, it can also be overwhelming at times, especially when we attempt to accomplish too much with our children and in our homes in a given day, week, or month.

It seems to me that the Lord must have had mothers in mind when he created the earth and separated the days by nights. Such a plan of separating the days by nights reminds us that we need to pause for rest and renewal. Such a plan can also serve as an invitation for us to stop at the end of each day to give thanks for the gifts of that particular day, to reflect on what we have done well on that day, and, if necessary, to seek forgiveness and to forgive ourselves for what we have not done so well. In other words, such a plan allows us to put yesterday to rest so we can awaken each morning to the gift of a whole new day—a day where we can focus on doing our best on just that particular day as we seek to raise and nurture righteous children.

Whether you are blessed to come from a long line of mothers who have raised their children in the gospel or are blessed to be the first mother in a family line to find and embrace the gospel, there is great joy to be had in wholeheartedly and thoroughly nourishing your own children in the gospel of Jesus Christ. As you strive to make the most of today and then tomorrow and the day after in teaching and guiding your children in spiritual matters, rest assured that the Lord will bless your efforts. And know this—that as you turn to the Lord and seek to raise your children within the gospel of Jesus Christ, you will be giving them a most precious and priceless inheritance. For you will be giving them the gift of having been taught by their mother, a mother who knows where to seek for spiritual power.

ABOUT THE AUTHOR

Debra Sansing Woods is a full-time mom and part-time freelance writer. Her writings often focus on and celebrate home and family life. Her articles have appeared in numerous publications, including *LDS Living, Meridian* magazine, two Deseret Book anthologies (as a contributing author), *The Dallas Morning News, The Athens Review,* and others.

Debra graduated from the University of Texas at Austin with a BBA in Accounting and went on to become a CPA and corporate controller. She also taught as a highly rated instructor of personal finance for the University of Texas Informal Classes. She currently lives in Oklahoma City with her husband, Barry, and their five youngest children. Debra's family also includes her husband's three grown daughters.

Photo by Jeffrey Adling